WESTMAR COLLEGE

W9-CBP-907

HERBART
&
EDUCATION

Studies in the
Western Educational Tradition

Consulting Editor
P A U L   N A S H • *Boston University*

HERBART
&
EDUCATION

Harold B. Dunkel
· University of Chicago ·

RANDOM HOUSE · NEW YORK

FIRST PRINTING

Copyright © 1969 by Random House, Inc.

All rights reserved under International and Pan-American
Copyright Conventions. Published in the United States
by Random House, Inc., New York, and simultaneously in Canada
by Random House of Canada Limited, Toronto.

Library of Congress Catalog Card Number: 69–10512

Manufactured in the United States of America.
Printed by Halliday Lithograph Corp., West Hanover, Mass.
Bound by H. Wolff Book Mfg. Co., New York, N. Y.

Contents

HERBART

&

EDUCATION

· I ·
Life

Johann Friedrich Herbart was born in Oldenburg, a town in Hanover near Bremen, on May 4, 1776. It was an exciting time to be alive, both culturally and politically. Goethe, Schiller, Kant, and Mozart were at the height of their powers and had already begun the great florescence of "German" culture, and Herbart was almost an exact contemporary of Beethoven, Schelling, and Hegel. Of the politically exciting nature of the period, Napoleon's birth in 1769 was a sufficient guarantee, and Herbart's mature years were passed amid the Napoleonic wars and the subsequent period of conservative reaction that spread across Europe after the Congress of Vienna in 1814–1815. Though he tried in general to ignore political matters, believing that they distracted him from his work, political events did impinge upon Herbart—when he was required to pay his part of the indemnities imposed by the victorious French, when students left his classes to enter the army, or when a reactionary regime affected his university. However much he wished to go his own way quietly, he could not escape the fact that he lived in tumultuous times.

Herbart's early home life and rearing left indelible marks on him. His parents were an oddly mismated pair. His father was the quintessence of the staid burgher. A state councillor, he moved happily in the narrow groove of home, office, and law court, desiring no greater excitement than a game of cards at his club in the evening. His hope for his son was merely that Johann would follow in his footsteps and lead the quiet life of a petty official in Oldenburg or some nearby town.

His mother was completely different. An active, energetic woman of strong will and firm determination, she was eager to see the world and to live life strenuously. The record seems to offer no plausible suggestion as to how this ill-matched couple ever came to wed, though it contains ample evidence that each found the other and the marriage highly unsatisfactory. Johann, as the only child of this unfortunate union, grew up in an unhappy household and lived amid continual strife between his parents until he finally left home for good at the age of twenty-four.

For Frau Herbart, who had found her husband stodgy and unresponsive, the birth of her son opened up new possibilities for exercising her intense drives, and during the following twenty years she concentrated all her efforts on him. This excessive concentration was first prompted when little Johann fell into a tub of almost boiling water. This accident presumably so impaired the child's health, particularly his eyesight, that it became the reason (or at least the excuse) for having him begin his education at home. Frau Herbart found a tutor and studied along with her son, even learning Greek in the process.

This tutor, Hermann Uelzen, like most of the tutors of the day, was a university product, waiting for a suitable opening in his specialty. (After leaving the Herbarts, he became pastor in the little town of Langelingen.) As a student of theology, Uelzen possibly stressed theology and philosophy more than a teacher who had specialized in law or philology would have done, and this bias may account for many of the topics on which the youthful Herbart wrote and spoke. But by and large, as far as we know, Herbart's early education was in most respects that of the middle-class boy of the time.

This choice of tutor appears to have been a very fortunate one. Though a theologian, Uelzen did not teach dogmatically or catechetically. Rather he seems always to have stressed the bases of proof and the grounds for doubt. In other words, particularly if compared with the customary practices of the day, Uelzen's general pedagogical method was essentially that of philosophic inquiry. The method was apparently effective, for Herbart, when he was twelve, made the transfer to the local Latin school without trouble.

His life up to the time of his departure for the University of Jena can be epitomized in the four following points, and all these elements will continue to run like threads throughout the fabric of his later life.

First, Herbart was both highly intelligent and hard-working. "Gifted," "intelligent," "diligent," and "industrious" are the sort of adjectives used to describe him as a schoolboy, and these same terms would appear in his obituaries. In addition to his conceptual abilities, he was an accomplished musician on several instruments, giving public performances and eventually even publishing a piano sonata.

Second, he possessed, thanks probably to the influence of Uelzen since neither parent is a likely factor, considerable interest and training in philosophy—we still have the outline of a paper he prepared at the age of thirteen on the proofs of the existence of an eternal God. As "firstboy" in the *Primar* or last year of the gymnasium, his congratulatory oration to the departing members of the preceding class was "Some Comments Concerning the Increase and Decline of Morality in States," and in the following year his Latin valedictory oration contrasted the views of Cicero and Kant concerning the supreme good. It is no wonder that in later years he felt himself a competent and practiced philosopher, entitled to philosophize in his own fashion despite the indifference and even the hostility of the public and his fellow philosophers.

Third, as an only child, tutored for a time in the home of mutually antagonistic parents and later as an intellectually precocious student younger than most of his classmates, Herbart always had trouble with casual personal relations. Relatively few people ever pierced the outer shell of apparent aloofness and austerity to find the inner man eager to make and keep friends. Once he did make a friend he held to him warmly and tenaciously, usually throughout life.

Finally, he was the victim of a close relation with his strong-minded, devoted mother, who had literally been his schoolmate and who would accompany him to the university and to his first job and would attempt to control him to the best of her ability. To protect himself against this onslaught, he seems to have developed a certain obstinacy that characterizes his personal and professional activities throughout his lifetime.

Such was the young man who in the summer of 1794 set out for the University of Jena, accompanied by his mother. Like most human motivation, Frau Herbart's was undoubtedly mixed. The excuse at this time once more was Herbart's poor health. But one suspects that she probably also hated to have this child, whom she had molded so carefully, escape her influence completely. Then too, accompanying her son gave her a chance to see more of the world and to escape for a time from her unpleasant marital situation. Certainly Frau Herbart seems to have enjoyed every moment of the physical and intellectual excitement of life in a university town. She became close friends with her son's professor of philosophy and his wife, the Fichtes, and reveled in sharing her son's life and his friends.

Presumably Herbart was to undertake the study of law in accord with his parents' wishes. But in his obstinate way he managed to begin by following his own preference for philosophy, and, possibly because of his mother's friendship with the Fichtes, he was allowed to pursue this course of study during his stay at Jena.

Philosophy was at that time a lively field in Germany, and in many respects the University of Jena had been the center of much of the activity before his arrival. The skeptical writings of David Hume had aroused Kant at the University of Königsberg from his "dogmatic slumbers," for it seemed to Kant that unless Hume's arguments could be met, science, metaphysics, and ethics as Kant conceived them were all threatened. Consequently, Kant had published in 1781 the first edition of what has been called the Doomsday Book of German philosophy, the *Critique of Pure Reason*, "in order to assign to reason her proper province." His subsequent contributions—the *Prolegomena to Any Future Metaphysics* (1783), the *Fundamental Principles of the Metaphysics of Ethics* (1785), the *Critique of Practical Reason* (1788), and the *Critique of Judgment* (1790)—had furnished additional powerful stimuli to German philosophy.

Although advancing age and the opprobrium aroused by *Religion within the Bounds of Reason Alone* (1793) had silenced Kant at Königsberg, his influence continued to remain strong at Jena. Erhardt Schmid as professor of philosophy had introduced the Kantian doctrines there very early, and Jena's *General Literary Journal* had been a major organ of the Kantian movement. This effect had been further reenforced at Jena during the professorship of Karl Leonard Reinhold, whose "Letters on the Kantian Philosophy" in the *German Mercury* had done much to spread Kantianism throughout German-speaking territory and whose interpretation of Kant had become the common "school version" of the doctrine, particularly at Jena. Reinhold left Jena just as Herbart came, but he was succeeded by Johann Gottlieb Fichte, who was to be Herbart's principal professor.

Fichte had started his philosophy from Kant's position. In fact, many had thought that an early work of his, which he had published anonymously, was the work of Kant. Kant had always insisted on calling his doctrine "critical philosophy" rather than "idealism." But his emphasis on the contribution that "mind" made to our knowledge of phenomena through its imposition of the forms and categories and the later efforts of his followers to solve some of the impasses in the Kantian system led most of the post-Kantians to various forms of idealism. Chief among these followers were Fichte and two of Herbart's contemporaries, Schelling and Hegel.

As Herbart said, Fichte tried to draw him into his manner of philosophizing; but the harder Fichte tried, the more Herbart moved from Fichte's idealism toward his own brand of realism. An important influence on Herbart in this regard was the publication of the fragments of Parmenides, the Greek philosopher who had conceived of being as consisting of simple atoms. To Herbart's view, the arguments of Parmenides and the paradoxes of Zeno, a later follower of Parmenides, made idealism untenable.

As Fichte's leading student, Herbart naturally became a member of the Association of Free Men, a student organization that Fichte and some of his colleagues were founding at Jena as an intellectual counterweight to the student-corps with their devotion to dueling and drinking.

The members and activities of the Association of Free Men overlapped to a considerable degree those of the Literary Society, whose members met regularly to read literary and philosophic papers they had written. In these groups the shy Herbart found his friends, and many of them were to be lifelong friends.

In 1797 one of the Swiss members of the society, Johann Fischer, was charged with finding a tutor for the children of the Landvogt of Interlaken, Karl Friedrich von Steiger. When Fischer consulted his Jena friends in his search for volunteers or suggestions, Frau Herbart urged her son to take the post. Though she had tolerated his presumably temporary defection from the study of law to philosophy, she was haunted by the fear that philosophy would never "earn bread." The job as tutor offered an opportunity to take him from the study of philosophy and introduce him to the world of work and pay. Herbart, however, demurred on the grounds that he was still far from ready to stand for his degree, which he planned to take at Göttingen, and that the job as tutor would only interpose further delay. But Mother insisted, and finally, as was usual, got her way and thus experienced what she called "the happiest day of her life."

Accordingly, in March 1797, Herbart, accompanied once more by Mama and by some friends from Jena, set out for Switzerland. The trip gave Frau Herbart further opportunity to prolong her absence from her unhappy home, to see the world, and to keep an eye on her son. But since she could scarcely settle in with the von Steiger family as cotutor, at Bern she turned back to her home and husband.

Herbart's charges were to be the two older von Steiger boys (there were two other younger boys as well as three daughters). He had formally agreed to stay with the household only for two years, but actually he came prepared to stay for eight or ten. Only over that long a period did he feel he could find sufficient time outside his working hours for his own intellectual labors before taking his degree and seeking an academic appointment. In addition to his great plans for his own projects, his work in the classroom would take six to eight hours daily, with additional time required for planning and preparation. Furthermore, his educational theories made him want to associate with the boys outside the schoolroom. As a result, only a prolonged stay would give him adequate time for everything he wished to accomplish both as tutor and scholar.

We know a good deal about Herbart's activities as a tutor, for every two months he filed a fairly long written report with Herr von Steiger, recounting the work he had assigned and the progress the boys had made; and five of these reports are extant. They clearly reveal the profound effect that this experience as a tutor had on all his later educational and psychological thought.

In this setting he first tried out many of the devices and procedures that he was to adopt and advocate for the rest of his life, such as the practice of beginning the study of the classical languages with Greek rather than with Latin. Similarly many of the examples, warnings, and conclusions of his later books are obvious echoes of experiences he first reported to Herr von Steiger or are partial portraits of the von Steiger boys. For example, Herbart thought that Ludwig, the oldest child, had already suffered from a deficient educational program; but in addition the boy was too indolent and too old and too reliant on his family's wealth and social position to be willing to do what was necessary to remedy his educational defects. As a result, we often find Herbart later admonishing other teachers to be prepared to do what he did then—scrap his planned program, lower his sights, and work out a new program fitted to the pupil's capacity and station in life. His relations with the second son, Karl, were much more rewarding, and they exchanged letters for years after Herbart had left the von Steiger household.

The most notable event of his stay in Switzerland, as one of his friends reported it, was that he "found his system." The university student of his time was as impressed by the knowledge-explosion of his day as we are by that of ours. The rise of German scholarship and the international expansion of science had produced a flood of new, exact knowledge in the humanities and in the sciences. The German student was expected to master much of this in the gymnasium and the university. Our modern response is to store and retrieve it electronically by computers. The technology of Herbart's day was limited to classifying it through building systems or organizations of the sciences.

These organizations attempted to classify and subclassify human knowledge in a conceptual structure where each item would have its specific, proper place. For example, the scheme of Francis Bacon is the basis for the familiar Dewey Decimal System used to classify books in many modern libraries. Since these organizations necessarily involved some explicit set of principles for separating yet relating the various fields—involving views concerning the nature of things, the kinds of knowledge, or the modes of obtaining knowledge—they tended to be fundamentally philosophic. The German student could adopt the scheme of some philosophic system congenial to him. Or, if he found none that he liked or if he had philosophic interests or pretensions as Herbart did, he might seek to evolve his own.

Herbart felt that the views current in his own day were wrong in many important respects. For example, he could not accept the metaphysics of Fichte and the contemporary idealists. Yet such views concerning the nature of things were usually important considerations in structuring knowledge. Likewise he considered the faculty-psychology of his day to be totally in error, yet psychological principles were likely to figure in any classification of knowledge. As a result, he felt under considerable compulsion to perfect a scheme of his own in which his new conceptions of metaphysics and psychology could be coherently related to the other fields of knowledge.

Herbart finally evolved his general plan in 1798, and he spent the rest of his life developing the specific parts of it in book after book. As far as we can ascertain, he made astonishingly few changes in this system in the following forty years.

Just how tightly his educational ideas were immeshed in this system has been the subject of some dispute during the past century. There can be no doubt that he himself saw his pedagogy as one of the "sciences," linked by precise and explicit relations to the other bodies of knowledge in the system. His many explicit statements to this effect cannot be simply ignored. Even without these assertions, since he lived in the age of the great system-builders, the presumption that he was "systematic" would be highly probable in any case. The question is whether he deceived himself into thinking that his educational ideas were more a part of this system than they in fact were.

The following chapters will proceed primarily on the principle that Herbart's educational views were actually a part of this total system. At very least, this is the way he said it was and probably the way he would have wished to be understood, yet the reasons for doubting the validity of this procedure should not be ignored. Consequently the grounds for thinking that perhaps he deceived himself about the closeness and necessity of the relations of his pedagogy to the rest of his system and the difficulties one encounters in attempting to treat Herbart as "systematic" in this fashion will be noted as they appear in the exposition, and the issue will be raised again in Chapter VIII.

One of these bits of evidence is constituted by the *Reports* just mentioned. As was noted, they contain many points that were always important parts of Herbart's educational theory. Yet they were written when his system was presumably at best still in embryo. This fact has led many to see the pedagogy as less tied to the system than he alleged and has even inclined some to regard the system as growing out of his pedagogical ideas rather than vice versa.

Whatever the facts of this situation, in 1898 Herbart, with what he considered the outlines of his future intellectual activity thus clear before him, was even more ready than before to prolong his stay in Switzerland. Tutoring provided at least an adequate living, and one surmises that life in the von Steiger household was far pleasanter and livelier than that which he had known in Oldenburg and which his parents expected him to resume someday. And clearly, though it must have cost considerable effort, he was managing to find time for study and thought along the lines of his own interests while discharging his tutorial duties.

But Herbart was on a tether, even though a long one. His parents, obviously only because he insisted so much, had allowed him to begin the study of philosophy. But apparently they both regarded this activity as merely a youthful fling. In their plans, sooner or later, with or without further training in law, he was to return home and take a post in the local bureaucracy. To keep this parental leash from being pulled short, he had saved part of his allowance during his student days as a reserve fund against being required to return home, as he might be forced to do if his parents reduced his funds. Probably he was also saving something from the monetary portion of the stipend from the von Steiger's.

His fears were realized shortly after he had discovered his system. A nobleman from Oldenburg was about to make an extended tour of Europe, and Herbart's parents had arranged for him to go along in the role of companion and then to return to a position in Oldenburg. Mother Herbart had even picked out a nice girl for him.

This contretemps demanded drastic countermeasures. Consequently, Herbart approached Herr von Steiger with a deal. If his employer was willing, Herbart would contract to remain for another eight to ten years—that is, until the education of the two younger sons was completed. In return he was to be assured of six weeks of free time annually solely for his own projects. Herr von Steiger agreed at once, and eventually even Herbart's parents consented.

Yet six months after all these arrangements had been made, Herbart gave up the whole idea. Although there were a number of possible excuses, such as his mother's illness and the increasing dissension between his parents, none of these proves adequate under scrutiny to explain his complete change of intent. Probably he simply could not sustain this complete revolt against his parents' wishes. In any case, April of 1800 found him in Oldenburg ready to do his parents' bidding.

But the gulf between his parents was too wide to be bridged even by Herbart's prostrate body. Frau Herbart, disappointed now both in her son and her husband, went off to see the world with a Dr. Harbauer, the personal physician of the king of the Netherlands; she was with him, in 1802 at Paris, when she died. (Few educators or philosophers have had mothers who tossed their caps over the windmill in this fashion.) This breakup of the parental household freed Herbart from the ties that had bound him for so long and permitted him to pursue the career of his own choosing, philosophy.

To this end he moved to Bremen and lived at the home and on the bounty of a friend of his university days, Johann Smidt. During his two years there, in addition to studying, Herbart did some tutoring, and some writing and lecturing on the work and writings of Johann Heinrich Pestalozzi, whom he had met when he first went to Switzerland and whose school at Burgdorf he had visited just before returning home.

In 1802 he went to Göttingen to take his degree, which he secured in October of that year. Deciding to continue there as a privatdozent until some salaried academic post should open, he realized that his metaphysics and psychology would be at odds with the popular schools of the times. Consequently he prudently began by lecturing on pedagogy and ethics.

In 1805 he received a call to Heidelberg as *professor ordinarius* (full or head professor) and another from Landshut six months later, but he refused both on the ground that Göttingen supplied more of what he wanted at that stage of his career. These offers, however, led Göttingen to appoint him as *professor extraordinarius* (associate professor).

At this time he began the activity that was to occupy much of the remainder of his life—the formal publication of the various parts of his system. He already had drafts for several parts of it; the only question was where to begin. In order not to lose the freshness of his educational activity and thought in Switzerland and Bremen, he decided to start with pedagogy. He published his *General Pedagogy* (translated into English as *The Science of Education*) in 1806 and followed it immediately with his *Chief Points of Logic* and the *Chief Points of Metaphysics.* In the next year his *General Practical* [i.e., moral] *Philosophy* appeared.

This spate of publications and his popularity as a lecturer made him conspicuous among the German professors of philosophy, and in 1808 he received a call as *ordinarius* to the University of Königsberg, to fill the vacancy left by Wilhelm T. Krug, Kant's immediate successor there, who had moved on to Leipzig. Since the chair was a distinguished one and offered the rank of *ordinarius* as well as four times his current salary, Herbart probably had an easy time deciding to accept.

His stay at Königsberg (1808–1833), his career from age thirty-two to fifty-seven, naturally enough contained many of the major events in his life. The first of these was the fight for his share in his mother's estate. Frau Herbart, with her fixed idea that philosophy could not earn bread, had put her estate in trust for her son until he reached forty-five, apparently on the ground that by that time he would have reaped the consequences of this youthful folly and would be in need of financial rehabilitation. Fortified by his appointment to Königsberg and aided by an old friend of the family, he managed to have the will set aside. He was then able to repay the loans from Smidt and other friends on whose generosity he had been living, and he was able also to have a small nest egg.

Another major event was his marriage to Mary Drake, an English girl. Her father had been a merchant in Memel, but impoverished by the war he had returned to England, leaving her (for reasons that are not clear in the record) living *en pension* at Königsberg. Herbart fell deeply in love with this girl, who was half his age, and married her in 1811 as soon as wartime communications permitted the necessary arrangements with her father and with her guardian in Memel. The marriage was apparently a happy one, and since it was childless, the young Frau Herbart could devote herself to her husband's activities.

Chief among these was the pedagogical seminar that he conducted during his entire stay at Königsberg. Believing pedagogy to be not merely a subject to be taught but also one to be demonstrated and practiced, he had asked that the official specifications of his appointment include both public lectures on pedagogy and the conduct of "practice exercises," as the seminar was originally called. His paradigm of the teacher (possibly because of his own experience both as student and tutor) was the tutor living in a private home with two or three children in his charge. As a result, the seminar provided experience more like practice-tutoring than like practice-teaching. Each student worked intensively in a few subjects with two or three children. These "guinea pigs" lived in Herbart's own home, a large house provided by his wife's capital and presided over by her; on occasion she served as house-mother for as many as thirteen such children. She also taught when student-teachers were lacking or when her command of English was needed.

Though the seminar achieved some outstanding results in educating these children (as revealed by the reports of the examining bodies brought in at Herbart's insistence), it was always a very small undertaking, and its procedures tended to justify the constant suspicion of the Prussian Ministry of Education that Herbart was using its subsidy to train tutors for private families rather than teachers for the Prussian schools. (The seminar was not continued after Herbart left Königsberg; both he and the university had had enough.)

More significantly, Herbart continued the publication of the parts of his system. The totally new ventures concerned psychology, a field that had always interested him and to which he gave most of his attention during his mature years. His major works in this area were the simpler *Textbook for Psychology* (1816), the larger and more complicated *Psychology as a Science* (1824–1825), and the *Letters on the Application of Psychology to Education* (1831). In all these he was trying to perfect a new, scientific, mathematical psychology to replace the faculty-psychology that he considered totally in error.

His publications were not, however, limited to psychology. In 1812 he had issued the first edition of his *Textbook for the Introduction to Philosophy*. He wrote this simply because his lecture hall was so crowded that students could not even find a place to sit—much less a proper place to take their own notes. This résumé of his general philosophic position was his most popular book, running through four editions. He also gave a much more complete treatment of his metaphysical views, summarized earlier in his *Chief Points of Metaphysics,* in the two volumes of his *General Metaphysics* (1828–1829).

Despite all this activity and achievement, Herbart did not acquire the fame and recognition he felt was his due. As the title of one of his minor monographs suggests, his entire professional life was a continual "struggle against the fashionable philosophies" of his day. The idealistic philosophies of Fichte, Schelling, and Hegel took Prussia and much of Europe by storm. Herbart's realism, whatever its merits or demerits, was clearly out of fashion. Though many students attended his lectures, they were not students of *his* doctrines, and he had relatively few disciples in any of the fields to which he made original contributions.

Yet he persisted. Having arrived at his philosophic views through prolonged and intensive thought and training, he felt that he would be a traitor to himself and to truth if he shifted his position merely to fit the times. Just as he had insisted on choosing and following his own career in the face of intense parental pressures, so he persevered in following his chosen philosophic course despite misunderstanding and slight.

The general unpopularity of his philosophical views is epitomized in the history of the chair of philosophy at the University of Berlin. When in 1810 Wilhelm von Humboldt established this new university, which for more than a century was for the world the model of the modern university, it was perhaps excusable that Herbart, already holding a post in Prussia, was not offered the position in philosophy. But later, when the chair in what had become the most prestigious German university was made vacant by the death of Hegel, clearly it was a slap in the face when Herbart, despite his best wirepulling, was passed over in favor of an unknown Hegelian.

Piqued by Prussia, Herbart resigned and returned to Hanoverian Göttingen, where a position providentially opened in 1833. With the publication of the second volume of his *General Metaphysics* in 1829, he felt that he had accomplished the major task of expounding his system. As a result the book-length products of the last years of his life at Göttingen were reworkings and extensions of positions already taken: the *Encyclopedia of Philosophy*

(1831), the *Outlines of Pedagogical Lectures* (1835), and
the *Psychological Investigations* (1839–1840).

These last years seem to have been as pleasant as they
could be for a man who had essentially missed his goal in
life—to be the foremost philosopher in Germany. He had
always been a popular lecturer. Now that he was devoting
less time to his own writing, he spent more time and effort
on his lectures, which were, as always, well attended. The
pleasant calm of these years was, however, marred by the
so-called Göttingen Catastrophe.

Hanover was at that time English territory. But at the
death of William IV of England, the Salic Law prevented
his female British successor, Queen Victoria, from ascend-
ing the throne of Hanover as well as that of England.
The rule consequently passed to the next in the male line,
her uncle, the Duke of Cumberland, a man said to have
been guilty of all the sins except suicide. As one of his
moves in the establishment of an absolute and conservative monarchy, the new ruler, under the title Earnest
August, abrogated the liberal constitution in 1833 and
demanded that all the state functionaries (a rubric including Göttingen's professors, of course) swear a new
oath of loyalty to him personally. Seven professors, object-
ing to the suppression of liberalism and to the new mon-
arch, refused to comply, and three of them were ultimately banished from Hanover.

Herbart, then the dean of the Faculty of Philosophy,
had urged compliance with the royal demand. Throughout his life he had had little interest in politics and had
paid little attention to them. Believing that peace and
quiet were essential if scholars were to pursue their intel-

lectual tasks, he thought it a mistake for the university to become embroiled in a struggle with the throne. This attitude did not endear him to his more politically active colleagues and students. But, as usual, he held to his own course. He merely recorded his side of the controversy in a brief monograph, which in accord with his instructions was published only after his death. The breach caused by this episode seems, however, to have healed in time.

Herbart lectured as usual on the morning of August 11, but in the evening he was stricken with a cerebral hemorrhage and died on August 14, 1841.

Herbart had been more than a run-of-the-mill university professor of his time. Unusually productive and creative, he had nonetheless encountered severe difficulties. One was that he was contending for the crown of German philosophy with some of the greatest philosophers Germany ever produced. To compete with Kant, Fichte, Schelling, and Hegel was no easy task, and to be a realist at the very *floruit* of German idealism did not make the struggle easier. The contrast served merely to place Herbart in a sort of philosophic underground.

Partly because of this position outside the mainstream of German philosophy and perhaps partly because of his difficulty in casual personal relations, Herbart had few devoted followers. Some he did have, to be sure, and men like Moritz Wilhelm Drobisch and Karl Volkmar Stoy kept his doctrines sufficiently alive for them to be revived later. But despite his popularity as a lecturer, he had no great personal following during his lifetime and made singularly little impression on the fields in which he worked, even including pedagogy, which was to be the primary scene of his later resurrection, in name at least. The rights and wrongs of this judgment of his contemporaries can be assessed only by examining his theories with that objectivity which the passing of time and fashion makes possible for us.

·II·
Herbart's System

Herbart saw his pedagogy as an integral part of his total philosophic system. As the preceding chapter indicated, he evolved the general structure of this system while he was still a tutor in Switzerland, and most of his subsequent writings are expositions of its details. He believed that his pedagogy was "nothing" without his metaphysics and ethics. Stating these relations more precisely, he asserted that education must find its ends in ethics and its means and hindrances in psychology. Presumably, therefore, if we are to understand his education theories in the way he intended, we must examine them in the context of his system, studying in some detail the parts most closely connected with education.

Through his system Herbart was attempting to organize what was considered the total field of philosophy in his day—that is, to show its major divisions and subdivisions along with the bases for the distinctions and relations between them. In his opinion, philosophy could not be defined by virtue of some distinctive subject matter that it studied, as botany might be defined as the study of plants or astronomy as the study of the heavenly bodies. The subject matter of philosophy seemed to him to be concepts, but these were studied by other sciences also. Philosophy then, he felt, must be characterized by the particular ways in which it handled concepts, and within philosophy its chief ways of treating concepts marked off its three major divisions.

First, Herbart thought, when philosophy began to work with concepts it sought to render them "clear and distinct." By that phrase he meant that philosophy marked off each concept from all others and determined precisely what it was. This clarification of concepts was the task of logic, the first of the major divisions of philosophy. Once logic had rendered concepts clear and distinct, then it could combine concepts into propositions and the propositions, in turn, into syllogisms and the other forms of inference.

Logic need not concern us in any detail for two reasons. First, Herbart had relatively little interest in the field since he thought the existing variety was adequate. Consequently, he attempted no new contribution of his own; his *Chief Points of Logic* is merely a conventional handbook intended primarily for the use of his students. Second, though logic was for Herbart certainly involved in education, it was less intimately connected than some other parts of the system. In sum, logic was relatively unimportant for his pedagogy and presented no special complications or novelty.

Herbart saw the second great division of philosophy as springing from a second way of treating certain concepts. When philosophy attempted to render certain important concepts clear and distinct, it discovered that upon this examination they were revealed as contradictory. For Herbart contradiction was a warning signal. The law of identity or noncontradiction must prevail. A rose must always be a rose and not sometimes a petunia. If *A* was sometimes *not-A,* if "up" was sometimes "down," rational thought and rational discourse seemed to him impossible.

Yet one of the tasks of philosophy is to explain our experience. But if philosophy talked about experience in contradictory concepts, it would say nothing clearly or else it would say one thing now, then something quite different later. To talk or think in this fashion was not philosophy as Herbart saw it. Philosophy had to employ noncontradictory concepts. Accordingly the task of metaphysics was to subject these contradictory concepts to a process of "reworking" (*Bearbeitung*) or "enlargement" (*Ergänzung*) in order to render them noncontradictory. This method of enlarging contradictory concepts was, therefore, the defining characteristic of Herbart's second major division of philosophy, metaphysics.

Metaphysics proper had a number of subdivisions, but as such they need not concern us here specifically. More important for our purposes is that Herbart saw metaphysics as capable of being applied; and three subdivisions arose, depending upon the material to which it was applied. If metaphysics was applied to the external world, the result was natural philosophy; if directed toward the internal world or mind, psychology; if toward the divine, natural theology.

In relation to Herbart's pedagogy, the situation of metaphysics—especially its applied subdivision, psychology—is quite different from the situation we saw for logic. First, he considered contemporary psychology to be completely in error, and he regarded his new mathematical psychology as his greatest contribution. Second, since psychology was to provide the technology enabling education to attain its ends, its connections with his pedagogy were presumably very close. Consequently, if we take his statements seriously, a detailed knowledge of his psychology is requisite for understanding his educational theory and practice. In addition to this knowledge of the applied branch, some familiarity with metaphysics itself is also needed. All his general metaphysics is not, however, relevant, but only those parts bearing most directly on the application to mind and providing the basic premises for his psychological theory.

The third major division of philosophy in Herbart's system arose from his belief that some concepts, once they are clear and distinct, are immediately accompanied by a judgment of "pleasing" or "displeasing." This field was aesthetics. In his thought in this division, he was much influenced by his knowledge of music, and he used a model taken from music.

A simple musical note is neither pleasing nor displeasing; it is merely a sound. But two or more notes struck together, a chord, are harmonious (pleasing) or discordant (displeasing). This fact suggested to him that aesthetics was not concerned with simple elements like single notes but with the relations between them.

A second point suggested to him by his musical analogy was that our reactions are immediate and intuitive; they are not reached by reasoning nor can they be proved. If someone asked why a harmonious chord is pleasing but a dissonant one displeasing, he felt there was no answer but "Listen!" In his opinion, as soon as the chord was heard, the judgment "pleasing" or "displeasing" immediately followed without further thought or feeling.

For Herbart, therefore, general aesthetics was concerned at the most general level with those relations which, when perceived, evoke from us the judgments "pleasing" or "displeasing." But obviously such a general theory was capable of a wide variety of applications and, like metaphysics, produced a number of more specific fields of applied aesthetics. These "doctrines of art," as Herbart called them, would instruct us how to act in certain areas if we are to win from spectators and ourselves the judgment "pleasing" rather than "displeasing." For example, the doctrine of art in regard to music tells us what chords and sequences would be pleasingly related. The corresponding doctrine in the graphic arts would reveal what relations of line, mass, and color would gain aesthetic approval.

Most of the doctrines of art, according to Herbart, gave us directions that were purely hypothetical. That is, they said that *if* one chose to operate in a given area in such a way that the result was pleasing, *then* one should relate the elements in this way rather than some other.

But we need not practice a particular art at all. For example, everyone did not need to compose music, or having tried his hand at it, a man could give up the art if he felt it was beyond his powers.

With one area, however, Herbart felt every man was necessarily concerned—moral actions and volitions. Therefore he considered the imperatives of this particular doctrine of art, practical philosophy, or ethics, to be categorical and not hypothetical. That is, man must will and act, and this activity must be of a certain sort if it is to gain moral approval.

Since the only kind of education in which he was interested was moral education, its ends rested on the Herbartian ethics. As a result, his ethical theory was a major determinant of his pedagogical theory, and his ethics must be understood if his educational theory is to be clear.

From this sketch of Herbart's total theory the situation of Herbart's pedagogy within it and the main lines of relation to other parts of the system should be apparent. These facts likewise indicate the amount of acquaintance the person interested in Herbart's educational ideas need acquire with the rest of the system. Ethics as revealing the aims of education is important and must be studied in some detail. Psychology, as specifying the machinery to be used and the difficulties to be surmounted in reaching this ethical goal, is equally important. The general metaphysics and general aesthetics as well as their other applied branches are much less relevant except as they figure in establishing the bases for ethics and psychology.

· III ·
Ethics

Since Herbart conceived the aim of education as morality, an understanding of his pedagogy demands some understanding of his ethical theory. Here, in contrast to his innovations in metaphysics and psychology, he did not seek for novelty. In fact, he felt that in a field that had been the object of philosophic reflection for so many centuries, innovation should be suspect.

At several important points his position was very similar to Kant's, whose *Fundamental Principles of the Metaphysics of Ethics* had impressed him deeply in his Jena days. First, he agreed with Kant that the basis of ethics lay in the goodness of the will. Thus the ethical problem was to define the "good" will, and the corresponding pedagogical task was to render the child's will good. Second, he shared Kant's desire to separate ethics from metaphysics, psychology, and anthropology. By making ethics a subdivision of aesthetics, he effected this divorce.

According to Herbart's aesthetics, judgments of "pleasing" and "displeasing" were not called forth by simple elements but only by relations between elements. Consequently, the ethical standards for the goodness of the will had to be criteria of relations of the will. He found five such internal and external relations, his "basic moral ideas."

The first of these he called "inner freedom." This relation was internal to each individual will and required that the two parts of the will be in harmony. One part of the will he called the "subjective" or "obeying" will; this was the will based on the inclinations, the passions and the desires—the physiological-psychological portion of the will. The second, "commanding" part of the will was that part responsive to the moral law—the moral will, rendering the aesthetic judgments of moral approval and disapproval. The will possessing inner freedom, therefore, would be the will that always willed in accord with the moral law. In his opinion this first idea was the fundamental expression of all morality, the summation of the proper relations in which the will should stand. Its name was, of course, a legacy from Kant. The will was internally free in that it was autonomous. It was not under an external or alien law; one part of it merely imposed its moral judgments on the other part.

The second basic ethical idea, "perfection," considered the strivings of the will simply as vectors, that is, as mere strivings without regard to the objects toward which the will happened to be directed. This idea concerned the forceful will, for Herbart believed that a will that did not will at all or willed only feebly was a contradiction in terms—a will that was not a will. In contrast, the will of Napoleon—a display of power just as is, for example, an earthquake—seemed to him to call forth our admiration even though the observer might deplore what was willed or the consequences of that volition; there seemed to him to be an aesthetic appeal simply in demonstrations of great volitional force.

This second idea thus illustrated what Herbart considered an important fact about all the moral ideas. Any one of them individually was wholly inadequate as a standard for morality; each must be conditioned and modified by all the others. Otherwise a one-sided morality or even immorality would result. So in this case, though he believed force in the will to be a desirable quality, this strength had to be directed toward good objects as judged by the other ethical ideas.

He further analyzed this concept of the forceful will into three aspects. The first of these, "intensity," considered only the strength of any single act of will. The second, "extension," concerned the number and variety of directions toward which these strivings went out. In his view, the truly strong will would not be devoted to merely a few objects but would go out toward many different ones. But lest this diffuseness dissipate the will, a third aspect of "perfection" was necessary. The intense and diverse strivings of the will had to be coordinated in a new totality of willing by "concentration."

Herbart's criteria for judging all three aspects of perfection had to be relative since he felt that no absolute standards of strength were possible. He was convinced, however, that if two wills were compared, an observer would always prefer the will with strong thrusts to one with weak thrusts, the will directed toward many objects to one with a narrower scope, and the will in which many strong strivings of various sorts were coordinated in an integrated pattern of volitions to one that was scattered and diffuse.

The third basic idea was "benevolence," a relation in which one will was kindly disposed toward the strivings of another will. Herbart regarded this relation as still internal to the first will, however, since no specific account was taken of the second will or of the objects toward which it strove.

The last two moral ideas, however, did take account of the other will and hence concerned a relation external to the first will. The fourth idea, "right" or "law," dealt with the case of two wills striving for the same object. Such a clash, if allowed to arise and to progress unchecked, would produce strife, a disharmony calling forth moral disapproval. On the contrary, recognition of the claims of law would produce a harmonious relation between the two wills and win moral approbation.

The fifth basic idea in Herbart's list was "requital," or "recompense." When "law" was violated, the exaction of just recompense would be morally approved, for the culprit would have got his just deserts. Herbart believed that giving renewed emphasis to this fifth idea was perhaps his sole contribution to ethical theory. The other four ideas had always been familiar in the history of ethical thought, but "requital," the basis of criminal law, had often been lost to view.

These then were the five relations characteristic of Herbart's "good" will. Though he believed it was impossible to demonstrate that this list was actually exhaustive, he felt that there was good evidence for its completeness. If one tried to find additional ideas by taking more wills into account, one merely added duplications of "right" and "requital." At the other end of the series, finding some idea beyond or behind "inner freedom" seemed impossible inasmuch as the concept of the obedience of the will to the moral law seemed the very definition of morality. For these reasons the list seemed to him complete and to organize comprehensively the entire field of ethics.

As was indicated earlier, Herbart insisted that the ideas could not be taken singly but must be used in combination to limit and condition each other. Thus "perfection" by itself could produce a will striving for the wrong ends or objects; "benevolence" without "perfection" would lead to a wishy-washy state of good intentions; "right" without "benevolence" would lead to a stern and rigid legalism; and so on. Both in assessing specific volitions and in judging human character in general, the five ethical ideas were to be used conjunctively.

Herbart saw only one possible way in which additional ideas could be obtained. That procedure was to postulate a society so integrated that it could be considered as possessing essentially a single will. Under these conditions, five parallel "social ideas" could be derived. Since a society would be involved, this list began with the social, negative (the avoidance of strife, the avoidance of injustice) ideas of "right" and "requital" of the first list and then moved backwards through the other three ideas.

That is, such a society would seek to avoid strife caused by the conflict of wills seeking the same object, and, parallel to the idea of "right" or "law," would set up a "system of law." Similarly, it would establish a "system of requital" through which the citizens would agree to abide by a set of punishments and rewards for observance and infringement of "right." On the more positive side, in accord with "benevolence" a society of this sort would seek to distribute the available goods equitably to all; for this purpose it would institute a "system of administration," and through it the benevolence of the individual would pass over into the mutual benevolence of all. But there are spiritual goods, so to speak, as well as material ones. Consequently, the idea of "perfection" would give rise to a "system of culture." Within it, "intensity" would seek to render through proper social arrangements the wills of all members equally resolute insofar as possible; through "extension" this society would strive to make each of its members sensitive to the actions and achievements of all the others, while "concentration" would be attained through the specialization of each member in his own vocation, though he would remain appreciative of the specialties of all the others. Finally, "inner freedom" would find its counterpart in the "ideal" or "ensouled" society, in which the collective will of all members would be obedient to the universal moral law.

These derived or social ideas were probably a reflection of the developing nationalism of the nations of Western Europe at the time. Prussia and some of the other states undoubtedly felt that they were approaching the situation suggested by these social ideas. But in the rather limited scope of his pedagogical works, Herbart made relatively little use of them.

His five basic ethical ideas, however, were major factors in determining his pedagogy. He saw the whole task of pedagogy as that of developing within the child a will that was good because it stood in these relations. The timing of his program was dictated in large part by the readiness of the pupil to understand and assimilate the various ideas, and he chose his materials and procedures ostensibly on the basis of the contribution they could make to this general objective. If we take Herbart's many assertions seriously, his ethics is in fact indispensable to his pedagogy. If the development of the good will were not the end of education, then his pedagogy would have relatively little that is new to say to us, and he would have been the first to assert this fact. He was well aware that education could seek other ends and that such ends would involve other means. For him, however, education was always directed toward moral development of the sort generally specified by the basic ideas.

Many of his alleged "followers" took "morality" in a very vague sense, not even specifying it to the extent suggested by the moral ideas. In extenuation of that position it may be argued that Herbart himself was not very specific. But this argument should be advanced only with a full recognition of his position and with a consideration of the degree to which these followers also occupied it. As his musical analogy made evident, Herbart's doctrine was a form of moral intuitionism. The aesthetic sense was to give immediate and infallible judgments concerning what was to be morally approved or disapproved. To a considerable degree, therefore, he undoubtedly felt that he need not go into particulars concerning what it was to be "benevolent" or the rest. Given the general concept involved in the moral ideas, the moral man could trust to his own aesthetic (moral) sense to determine whether a given action was or was not benevolent. More precise statements could have been at best general guidelines. The actual touchstone was always for Herbart the aesthetic judgment, which each properly educated man always had at his disposal.

·IV·
Metaphysics

Many parts of Herbart's general metaphysics and two of its applications, natural philosophy and natural theology, have relatively slight bearing on his educational theory and practice. The student of his pedagogy can, consequently, slide over them rather casually or omit them entirely. But the third of the applied fields, psychology, was, at least according to Herbart himself, indispensable to an understanding of his pedagogy. As a result, an examination of that part of metaphysics most involved in its application to the internal world, the metaphysics of mind so to speak, demands some consideration.

As was indicated in the sketch of Herbart's system in Chapter II, he saw the function of philosophy as that of explaining human experience. When we begin to think about human experience, said Herbart, we use concepts. Hence came that preliminary task of philosophy assigned to logic, the job of rendering our concepts clear and distinct so that they can be useful tools in the service of thought. But in his opinion some of the concepts traditionally most used to deal with experience proved to be contradictory and hence inadequate to the task of explaining experience. His metaphysics, consequently, undertook to "enlarge" or "rework" those concepts in such a way as to remove or avoid the contradiction.

Four concepts that had figured most prominently in metaphysical thought seemed to Herbart to commit this sin of contradiction: "substance," "self" or ego, "change," and "matter." Their contradictory quality seemed to him to suggest not only why they had been the traditional pivots on which metaphysical thought and discussion had turned, but also why metaphysics had failed to produce a generally satisfactory explanation of what is given in experience. For example, Herbart disagreed with his teacher, Fichte, because Fichte used one of these concepts, the ego, as the basis of his entire system. As a result, Fichte's thought seemed to Herbart to be mired from the very outset in contradiction.

Since these concepts were contradictory, they could not become clear and distinct. A was sometimes A but sometimes not-A. Consequently, metaphysical discussions of any one of them tended to wander off into a discussion of one or more of the others. Since they and their mutual relations were obscure, metaphysical discussion, which turned on these concepts, had inevitably been, it seemed to him, ill-organized and inconclusive.

Since Herbart saw the task of philosophy as that of explaining human experience, he thought that metaphysics should begin by asking what was in fact given to us by experience, what there was to be explained. The common-sense answer to these questions was "things, objects." And what knowledge does experience give us about these things? asked Herbart. None. Experience tells us only about the qualities or characteristics of things, not about things as they are in themselves. Indubitably these characteristics seem in some sense to be "given" us in experience since we cannot change our perceptions of them by some act of will. Things do appear to us as having these qualities. And two points about these qualities of things as they appear to us were most important for Herbart: the qualities are numerous and they are subject to change. The piece of iron appears heavy, red, hot, and has a lot of other qualities; but in a little while it may be heavy, black, cold, and have other qualities, both similar to and different from those which formerly appeared to us.

But what, asked Herbart, do we know about those "things" with which we began as the items given us in experience? Nothing except this list of qualities that they are alleged to possess. In his view, metaphysics had merely hypothesized a "substance" or substrate in which the qualities could "inhere," something to give them a temporary local habitation. But metaphysical thought never talked about the thing, *A*, he insisted, but only about its characteristics, now perhaps *a*, *b*, and *c*; but then, later, perhaps *b*, *f*, and *g*. In short, *A* is not one thing, *A*, but many things; moreover it is not always the same "many," for at one time it possesses certain qualities; at other times, others. This state of affairs was for Herbart a clear violation of the law of identity, a contradiction.

The same situation seemed to him to arise in connection with another pivot, the self. What does experience reveal to us about the self? Nothing about the self as self. The alleged "self" is merely a cluster and succession of states of mind, perceptions, feelings, and the like. It is not one clear concept, but only a cluster of qualities, all of which are subject to change. To talk about the "self" as a "subject" is merely to use the word in the subject-position in such propositions as "——is sad," "——perceives green," "——feels pain."

Even this casual examination from Herbart's viewpoint of only two of the traditional pivots of metaphysical thought should indicate the sort of thinking that led him to his ultimate metaphysical position. Since these traditional pivots struck him as contradictory, he resolved to make a fresh start by searching for concepts that would not suffer from such shortcomings as did "substance," "change," "self," and "matter."

He believed that he had found the clue in the theory of Parmenides, who saw being as simple and unchanging. Accordingly, he postulated a universe of simple "reals," as he called them. Each real was a single, simple, unchanging quality. In this way there was no question of qualities "inhering" in a "substance," since each real was simply a quality; its being or substance *was* that quality. The paradoxes and perplexities of how a thing possessed of one set of qualities could turn into something else possessed of a different set were avoided inasmuch as the reals were unchanging. In short, the reals were the embodiment of the law of identity. Real *A* was always *A*; real *B* was always *B*, and so on.

This postulation of a world of simple reals, without parts, without change, unrelated to time and space, achieved Herbart's purpose of beginning with noncontradictory concepts, but such a world is definitely not that given to us in experience. Herbart then had to face the questions: "How can what we know as human experience arise from such beginnings?" and "How does experience come to be what it is?" In other words, how can this world of simple, unchanging reals produce that experience we have of things possessing many changing qualities in time and space?

To answer these questions Herbart's next step was to postulate that some reals are souls or are endowed with soul. This statement involves a number of difficulties, and, since it is the basis of Herbart's psychology, it must be examined with some care.

But first the advantages that Herbart gained by starting in this way should be noted. For one, by making the soul a real that had no relation to time and space, he avoided all the contemporary religious controversy about the immortality of the soul. The soul never ends temporally because it is not in time at all. The second advantage gained by the postulate was that through providing a soul it furnished a locus in which human experience could occur. No such events are possible in the world of the simple, unchanging reals. This second related advantage existed in large part because of the wide range of meanings traditionally attached in the Indo-European languages to the word "soul." To the Greeks, at the dawn of philosophic thought, *psyche* was not merely the religious word for "soul" or "breath of life," but also, as the word "psychology" shows, the word for "mind." Herbart, then, by using "soul" as well as the equally ambiguous German word for "spirit" or "mind" (*Geist*) covered both religious and psychological territory.

Yet the difficulties involved in this postulate were enormous. To say that some reals are "soul" seems difficult, for "soul" or "mind" hardly seems a simple quality like "redness"; and yet the reals are to be simple qualities. A simple unchanging real is not a very likely habitation for the varied contents of mind or the kaleidoscope of human experience. Or to look at the problem the other way around, how can the variety of human experience or the varied contents of mind be equated to a simple unchanging quality? Similarly, to say that some reals are "endowed with mind," or "possess mind," or are "minded" seems even more difficult than to say that they "are mind." If a real is to be only a simple quality, it can hardly possess anything else except that simple quality which is its being. Otherwise it is no longer simple, but is a quality *plus* soul or mind.

Since simple answers to the problem seem impossible, students of Herbart have attempted to evolve more elaborate ones. But the germ of the problem is apparent in these simple statements of it, and more elaborate solutions tend to obfuscate the difficulty rather than actually obviate it. To put the matter bluntly, Herbart was going to have trouble in moving from his noncontradictory, unchanging reals to the shifting, contradictory, paradoxical world of human experience.

For the moment, however, we must return to that world of the reals, for even if Herbart had in some fashion arrived at the point of positing mind, he had as yet provided it with no content, no experience. He had to find some metaphysical basis for the variegated contents of mind, the changing flow of consciousness.

He sought to provide this metaphysical ground through his theory of the "coming and going" of the reals. Since the reals were postulated as not in time or space, this activity could not be a literal, spatio-temporal coming and going. As he pointed out, he had to use the ordinary words of time and space to suggest a kind of association and disassociation for which language provided no adequate terms. This attempt to enliven the placid world of the reals by the postulation of their coming and going had extensive consequences and encountered some formidable difficulties.

Herbart further postulated that with the "coming together" of two reals two additional processes occurred. Each real sought to destroy the other, that is, to impose its own quality upon the other. But since, by the original postulate, each real remained forever just what it was, this attempt at destruction was frustrated and remained nothing more than a "perturbation" (*Störung.*) For in the face of this perturbation exerted by the first real, the second real generated an exactly equivalent amount of "self-preservation" (*Selbsterhaltung*). As a result, both reals continued as before.

Herbart's reason for postulating these perturbations and self-preservations is, of course, quite clear. Unless the world of the reals was shaken up in some fashion nothing would happen, and human experience would never occur. Yet, as before, this additional postulate was not added without difficulty. If it is the nature of the reals to be a single simple quality, the tendency to destroy or disturb can hardly be this same quality but is something in addition to it. This is also true of the tendency or capacity for self-preservations. In both cases something new seemed to have been added to the simple nature of the reals, which were presumably constituted solely by their being some one quality. The real would then become a complex entity rather than a simple being.

Herbart, admittedly, did not worry about this difficulty. Or perhaps he felt he could not. He had to agitate the tranquil world of the reals in some fashion if anything more than the unchanging persistence of simple qualities was to occur. Possibly this way of gingering up the situation seemed the least of the inevitable difficulties. More probably, perhaps, he did not see this postulate as a difficulty because of the nature of his model. As will be evident from his psychological theory, Herbart was much impressed by the contribution of Newtonian mechanics to the development of the physical sciences. To make use of this model, consequently, he claimed that it was often useful to consider as forces both the reals and the presentations (*Vorstellungen*) or ideas, even though he recognized that they were not in fact forces at all. In the present instance, he apparently regarded the perturbations and self-preservations of the reals as the analogy of two equal weights on a balance. Each continues to exert its own gravitational force unchanged, but because they are counterpoised, nothing happens: the beam of the scale does not move.

If these difficulties could be ignored and the coming together of reals taken as producing perturbations and corresponding self-preservations, then Herbart had a source for the contents of mind: The ideas or presentations in mind were the by-products of those acts of self-preservation performed by the soul when perturbed by the presence of another real. The soul was, so to speak, a seismograph reflecting in its presentations its acts of self-preservation in the face of perturbations.

At this point one may ask why Herbart bothered about all this. Critics have felt that he worried about thus establishing a basis for his psychology simply because of his metaphysical predilections and interests. They have justly pointed out that as a psychologist he could have simply begun with the ideas as given, without worrying much about their origin. It is also true that he operated in essentially this fashion once he began to develop his specifically psychological doctrine. His efforts to base psychology on metaphysics do, of course, indicate his effort to be comprehensively systematic. If he was to talk about mind, he wished to be clear about its metaphysical status. But there were also epistemological questions. He was too close to the work of Kant and Hume to be prepared merely to take ideas as ideas, as isolated phenomena of an internal world. He felt impelled to ask what relation they had to the external world, to inquire what they were ideas *of*.

Naive realism had been content to say that sense impressions were the direct copies of objects in the external world. The work of Kant, by emphasizing the contribution that the perceiving and thinking subject made to his own perceptions and thoughts through the inevitable involvement of his perceptual and conceptual mechanisms, had rendered the easy answer of naive realism unacceptable to Herbart. In seeking to rehabilitate realism, or at least to make it more sophisticated, he felt obliged to take account of Kant's position.

For Kant the objects of the external world were forever unknowable as they are in themselves; what we know are phenomena, things as they appear to us when structured by the forms and the categories imposed by human sense and reason. In some respects Herbart's position was similar to Kant's. For Herbart the immediate ground of our knowledge was the presentations, those side effects of the soul's efforts at self-preservation. They do not, therefore, come into mind from the outside nor do they give us direct knowledge of the external world, that is, of the reals whose perturbations give rise to the soul's self-preservations and hence to its ideas. In this sense the reals are Kantian things-in-themselves, forever unknowable. They were hypothesized merely to account for phenomena. Yet something appears to us in experience, Herbart insisted, and even if our knowledge is, as Kant had claimed, limited to these appearances or phenomena, Herbart felt that it was fair to ask, "What appears in appearances even if we cannot know these elements of reality as they are in themselves?" His attempt at a noncontradictory answer was to postulate the reals.

At this point too his scientific models influenced him

strongly. In astronomy the sun and the planets *appear* to move around the Earth, and in parts of their paths the planets *appear* to have a retrograde motion. But, Herbart pointed out, astronomers had not been limited in their knowledge to these appearances. They had been able to get behind the apparent motions to the real ones. Herbart wanted epistemology and metaphysics to follow a similar program.

For him ideas were not copies or pictures of the reals. They do not tell us what reality is like if by "reality" we mean what those simple qualities are that constitute the being of the various reals. What the presentations do convey, he thought, was knowledge of the *relations* between reals.

Precisely what he meant by this is possibly easiest to see if we revert to one of the traditional metaphysical pivots, substance. Substance had been hypothesized as an abiding substrate in which those characteristics which are all we know of things could inhere. Substance could, consequently, appear to change as now one set of accidental qualities inhered, now a different set. Herbart explained this change in the appearance of things in a rather similar way through his theory of the coming and going of reals.

According to the traditional theory, things had an apparently abiding or fixed quality because of the permanence of substance. Said Herbart, this abiding nature of a thing was due to the continued presence of a single central real. The seemingly changing characteristics were caused by the comings and goings of other peripheral reals. In this way, he believed, presentations were indicative of "what truly happens," of "real events," in that they gave us knowledge of the relations between reals (i.e.,

their comings and goings) but not knowledge of those actual qualities constituting the being of the reals. According to Herbart's theory, if a bar of iron becomes hot and
red, it is because new reals become associated with the
group called "a bar of iron." But the observer's perception
of "heat" and "redness" does not mean these are the actual
qualities of the reals giving rise to this perception. Our
knowledge is only of the relation, not of the basic qualities.

The foregoing is a very small portion of Herbart's
metaphysics, selected on the basis of its relevance to his
psychology and hence to pedagogy. It is, however, a fairly
representative sample of his general method of working,
the elaborateness of his metaphysical machinery, and the
clumsiness and generally unsatisfactory nature of some of
that apparatus. But the reader who is interested in Herbart's metaphysics primarily for its bearing on pedagogy
can be spared most of the complications.

·V·
Psychology

In his metaphysics Herbart had established by postulation that some reals had minds or were in fact minds. In response to the perturbations exerted by other reals, these ensouled reals exhibited equal acts of self-preservation, which became the presentations in mind. These were the metaphysical bases of Herbart's psychology. As a result, presentations did not come into mind from without, nor were they the products of mind itself. They were the consequences of the acts of self-preservation of the soul.

Herbart was in fundamental disagreement with the psychology of his day. He had no patience with that faculty-psychology which believed that ideas were received by the sensibility, recorded by the memory, ordered by the reason, and so on. That view seemed to him a pure mythology of the doings of psychic spirits. On the contrary, his view was that mind was not a congenital structure of faculties, capacities, categories, innate ideas, or anything else of the sort; rather its structure was acquired through experience, built by and out of the presentations arising in it. Its structure and its content were both products of those consequences of the soul's encounters with other reals.

A number of lines of thought led Herbart to this general position. Certainly one was the deep impression made on him by contemporary studies in anthropology. To say that Immanuel Kant and a Bushman both possessed the same faculty or capacity for reason, and that it was merely developed highly in one and not developed in the other, seemed to Herbart absurd. He was convinced that no empiricist could demonstrate the existence of reason in the Bushman and that the culture in which Kant had grown up had not merely developed his reason but had actually implanted it.

Another reason for taking this view was what he felt was the lesson taught by the growth of the natural sciences. They had all begun with a "natural history" phase in which single specimens and single observations had been painstakingly collected. Only after this basic stage had been fairly well completed had they turned to developing more complex concepts like "species," "class," or "law." Psychology seemed to Herbart to have worked in the opposite, and probably wrong, direction by beginning with what he regarded as very complex and elaborate concepts like "faculties" or "capacities." Although he was disposed to admit that the proper basic elements for psychology "did not lie obviously at hand," he felt that they were the points at which psychological inquiry should begin. These basic elements would have to be found, or, if they could not be found, would have to be postulated. The presentations as suggested by his metaphysics seemed to him plausible candidates for the role of such elements.

Still another influence that probably moved him toward this general position was the nature of the model he wished to follow. Seeking to make psychology a science, he took Newtonian mechanics as the paradigm of what science was at its best, and he tried to build an analogous statics and mechanics of mind. Two things in particular struck him about the Newtonian model: it was mathematical and it was based on what Herbart called "fictions."

A body in uniform rectilinear motion with no other body to affect its speed or direction obviously exists nowhere. It is a fiction. But by using such a fiction as his first law, Newton had revolutionized physics and astronomy. Likewise, "points" and other mathematical elements did not exist; yet mathematics was the basis of all "real" science. By using analogous procedures, Herbart hoped to become the Newton of psychology.

His procedure in metaphysics should have prepared us for what he did. There, though the reals were not to be taken literally as forces, he had suggested that they be considered *as if* they were forces. On this basis he had treated the reals as opposed to each other and as exerting perturbations and self-preservations, thus giving rise to the presentations. It was scarcely surprising, therefore, that in his psychology he wanted to begin by considering the presentations as if they too were forces.

Then, still guided by Newtonian thinking, he could begin with the simplest possible imaginary situation in which one presentation already in mind was confronted with another presentation. Treating them as opposing forces, he could then calculate what the consequences of this encounter would be. Next he could consider what would happen thereafter if these two presentations, now an interacting system or "apperceptive mass," were to be met by a third presentation, and they in turn by a fourth, and so on. In grossest outline this was Herbart's program for his psychological investigations.

This view that mind was built up out of the presentations arising in it, with the existing structure continually altered by new presentations and with the new elements also modified by the existing structure they encountered, was Herbart's theory of apperception. The term "apperception" and some of the concepts had their origins in Leibnitz and Kant; but Herbart's development of the doctrine is so much his own that a historical survey of its roots would be more of a digression than an aid in understanding it.

To be "scientific" meant for Herbart primarily to be mathematical, and in his view the task of psychology was to produce mathematical descriptions of the encounters between presentations and masses of presentations. As a result the pages of his psychological works are liberally besprinkled with the calculus as various situations are set forth mathematically and the consequences computed. But the main features of Herbart's psychology are perfectly accessible apart from the mathematical apparatus, and they are the points the follower must accept and the critic refute; the mathematics is neutral. Nevertheless, anyone wishing to get the real feel of Herbart's psychology should glance at some of the psychological works in the original, even one having no knowledge of mathematics or German. Only in this way does the main thrust of Herbart's effort become fully apparent.

Let us begin with the simplest encounter, that between the first two presentations occurring in mind. The two presentations—like two reals, like two forces—would in general oppose each other; but precisely what happened would depend on several factors. First, Herbart distinguished three categories of presentation: "similar," "dissimilar" (or disparate), and "contrary." The similar presentations could blend into fusions (*Schmelzungen*) or very tight combinations. Dissimilar ones, because of their very lack of similarity, would form less closely knit combinations, "complexions" (*Complexionen*). In the case of two contrary propositions, it would be war; the stronger would succeed in wiping out the weaker in exact proportion to the extent it was stronger.

By this point the reader who is used to theory-building is likely to inquire what was meant by "similar," "stronger," and the rest and to ask how the variation in these qualities was measured. Herbart offered essentially commonsense or common-language answers. Colors were similar simply because they were all colors. Thus red and blue combined to make purple, a fusion; more red made the purple more reddish while more blue made the purple more bluish. In short, if one asked what made things "similar," Herbart answered in terms of class nouns: colors, smells, sounds, and so on.

Consequently colors were "disparate" from sounds, and so on, and the complexions they formed behaved quite differently from the fusions. For instance, adding more barking to a black dog does not change the blackness and vice versa.

In the case of the contrary presentations, the examples were the standard ones: hot/cold, wet/dry. The consequence was either heat or cold depending on the relative strength of the presentations involved. Sometimes this measure of strength was essentially mechanical and hence easily open to quantitative measurement—even though Herbart did not himself attempt it. Ice will cool boiling water or the water will melt the ice largely as a function of the quantity of each in a given case. That a clap of thunder would be louder than the buzzing of a bee could be measured in decibels. Accordingly we are not surprised when we find that Herbart the pedagogue liked choral recitation on the ground that it produced a "stronger" presentation than a single voice. But measuring strength was usually not that simple. For example, Herbart believed that the teacher who presented a story in an "interesting" fashion made a "stronger" presentation than one who told the tale dully. Measurement of the variables here would be more complicated. In any event, he did not undertake it.

A postulational system demands that it be checked by deducing empirical consequences from it. In this direction Herbart tended to go no farther than to cite examples like those just given to demonstrate that his system did make sense. Red and blue do act in this way to form purple, don't they? This casual sort of empirical check tended to suffice for him. And if one asked why the presentations combined in their various fashions rather than stand separate and isolated as did his reals, he would probably have offered the empirical fact of the unity of consciousness. Since this unity was, he believed, clearly given in experience, it had to be accounted for, and he believed that treating the presentations as combining or opposing forces explained it plausibly.

Herbart began with the simplest situation involving only two presentations merely to lay the groundwork for greater complexities, but even in this situation he found one point of interest. Regardless of the relative strengths of the two presentations, the stronger could never completely arrest (*hemmen*) the weaker; that is, the equation would never give the value o for the weaker presentation. But two forces combining against a third could drive it down below the "threshold of consciousness." By that expression Herbart meant that in the equation the value for that presentation worked out to o. He definitely did not mean that the presentation was annihilated, for in his view nothing in mind was ever totally lost. Nor did he mean that the presentation was "lost to consciousness," since he was careful to point out that "that presentation is in consciousness or above the threshold of consciousness" was not the same as "I am conscious of that presentation." Rather he meant that a presentation below the threshold of consciousness had lost all its "force"; it was no longer effective in shaping the content of mind above that threshold.

But presentations always sought to remain above the threshold. Just as Herbart considered a will that was fit to be called a will would will strongly, so a presentation, as a force, was always ready to assert itself—that is, to remain above the threshold, or, if thrust below it by arrest, to rise above it again as soon as circumstances permitted. Mind was always in motion—a proposition he felt was proved by the fidgeting of small boys.

The more complicated mental situations were those where instead of one presentation encountering one or two others, a presentation or group of them met another mass or row. In these cases Herbart's general principle was that similar individuals or groups united and thus assisted each other in remaining above the threshold of consciousness or in rising above it again if some of them had sunk below it. In other words, a new presentation appearing and finding no similar presentations already in mind, would be arrested by the dissimilar or contrary ones it did find and thus sink below the threshold. If, however, a new presentation found similar ones already massed in mind, it would be immediately bound in with them and thus supported above the threshold. Likewise a presentation or group of presentations that had sunk below the threshold was assisted in rising above it by the appearance of similar presentations above the threshold. (This rising was also possible if the suppressing presentations were, in their turn, arrested by others and thus the presentations formerly suppressed by them could rise.)

This phenomenon of rising involved two processes that were important for Herbart: "vaulting" (*Wölbung*) and "pointing" (*Zuspitzung*). Let us say, for example, that a group of presentations lying below the threshold of consciousness consists of the recollections of someone I have met. If I have met him only once, and he and his appearance had no similarity with anything in my existing apperceptive mass, they would naturally sink below the threshold of consciousness, arrested by the dissimilar or contrary masses already present. But when I meet him again, all the items of his appearance are pulled up from the other presentations lying below the threshold of my consciousness, attracted by the similarities in his appearance on both occasions. But the more similar or identical presentations (his features, hair color, etc.) are pulled higher than the less similar ones (e.g., his clothing on the earlier occasion). Thus while all the elements connected with him rise somewhat higher than all the other items below the threshold ("vaulting"), the more similar ones are pulled higher, thus producing an apex on the vault ("pointing"). As a result, the more frequently the man and I meet, the more quickly and easily I recall those things that are truly characteristic of him, that are similar on all these occasions (build, feature, voice, walk), even though I may not recall the dissimilar elements (what he said or what he wore in each instance).

This general mechanism was, of course, for Herbart the process through which concepts or general ideas developed. As particulars are encountered time after time, their identical (essential) elements are subjected to repeated pointings and thus become clearer and clearer. Thus the general concept begins to form as a cohesive apperceptive mass. The incidental or accidental qualities, however, though occasionally participating in the general vaulting, do not receive so much pointing and hence do not enter into the mass that ultimately constitutes the clear general idea. A general idea is built up in this way like a composite photograph.

In Herbart's psychology the feelings, the desires, and the will did not have separate origins but were also products of this interplay between presentations. Some feelings, for example, arose from the union or clash of presentations. An easy fusion produced a feeling of pleasure; a clash of contraries, however, gave rise to displeasure. But feelings in what Herbart felt was the true sense of the term were connected with the rising of presentational masses. The rising of a mass assisted by the appearance of a new similar mass gave rise to a feeling of pleasure. If, however, this rising was partially checked by ties the older mass had to other masses, then the feelings were painful. To use Herbart's example, the sight of an object belonging to a dead friend tends to raise the mass of presentations connected with him; but at the same time the thought of his death tends to repress the thought of him, and this counterpull produces painful feelings.

Herbart saw desires as very closely connected with feelings. Let us take the situation just given in which A (the friend) is recalled by the presence of C (the object) but is simultaneously repressed by B (the thought of his death). The general formula is then: the recall of A with the aid of C is hindered by B. If B is weak, however, A will be raised above the threshold of consciousness by the pull of C; but the feeling of effort that overcomes the resistance of B will constitute a desire, and A will be active in consciousness as an object of desire.

Though Herbart saw the origins of both feelings and desires in the presentations, they seemed to him to differ in several important respects from other apperceptions. Most important, they were less persistent. In his view, they were not bound into general apperceptive masses as were most presentations, but were attached to specific presentations. As a result, they rose and sank with those particular presentations. As he put it, the old man no longer feels the joys and sorrows or the desires of his youth, but what he learned as a schoolboy he still knows. Likewise, because feelings and desires were not bound into large apperceptive masses, Herbart felt that several of them, even contradictory ones, could exist in consciousness side by side. On this point once again he appealed to what was given in experience. Since there is a unity of consciousness, the presentations must blend; but experience shows that we can simultaneously have conflicting desires; hence they must be capable of coexistence.

The will for Herbart was essentially the same as the desires, the distinction resting on the attainability of the object involved. In the terms of Herbart's own example, what Napoleon willed as emperor he merely desired as a prisoner on St. Helena. In other words, as we saw in regard to the ethical ideas, Herbart's will had objects for its strivings. If they were attainable, then the effort was a striving of the will. If they were unattainable, the effort was merely a desire.

Even this cursory sketch of Herbart's psychology should indicate the relevance he saw in it to pedagogy. A lesson (i.e., a new presentation or mass of presentations) appearing in mind would simply sink below the threshold of consciousness unless united to other similar presentational masses. As we shall see, this was where the famous "steps" came into play. They were to link each new item of subject matter to existing masses in mind by explicitly showing their relatedness. New learning had to be related to old. Otherwise the teacher would waste his time by merely dropping into mind, so to speak, material that would immediately sink below the threshold of consciousness and lie inert. The development of great apperceptive masses was also the means of achieving the great aim of education, moral strength of character, for only large, stable apperceptive masses could produce consistent and persistent states of character.

But the problems already noted in regard to "similarity" and "strength" will reappear. For example, as we shall see, Herbart strongly believed in using Homer's *Odyssey* in the original Greek very early in the boy's education. It might seem as if the doings of Greek heros about 800 B.C. as recounted in a foreign language would be very "dissimilar" to the experience of a German boy of A.D. 1800. But here Herbart saw great similarity both in the "boyishness" of the Greek heroes and in the level at which they posed and solved their moral problems. These similarities seemed to him to far outweigh the differences. Other examples could be adduced. The notable fact is that here Herbart undertook no empirical testing or measurement of "similarity" or "dissimilarity" beyond the pragmatic test that the *Odyssey* had proved usable with his pupils. He merely asserted the similarity or dissimilarity; and, if the materials worked to his satisfaction in the schoolroom, that was that.

This procedure is one of the facts giving rise to the suspicion that he was actually much less systematic than he alleged. That is, it is possible to suspect that Herbart's educational program was largely developed from his pedagogical theory and pedagogical experience and not out of his psychological theory. This view would then hold that his pedagogy was not derived in any sense from his psychology but rather that his psychology was merely called in to justify what he would have done anyway for other reasons.

·VI·
Pedagogy

The only kind of education in which Herbart was interested was moral education. Though he acknowledged that education could serve many other purposes, such education did not interest him. For him the fundamental problem of education was how to make the pupil a moral being, one possessing a good will. All the materials and procedures of education were to be selected and judged on the basis of their contribution to this one end, morality.

But morality was complex, for he saw it as specified by the five basic ethical ideas, all of which mutually conditioned each other. And each was also complex individually inasmuch as, for example, one could be "benevolent" in many different ways. Where was the teacher to begin?

The way out of this perplexity, Herbart thought, was to look at the pupil and see what each stage of his development made possible or required; the teacher could then determine what resources he could muster to this end.

Herbart divided pedagogy into three related divisions: "government" (*Regierung*), "discipline" (*Zucht*), and "instruction" (*Unterricht*), each division representing a general sort of activity in which the teacher would engage in his effort to induce morality in the child. This listing is in order of increasing complexity and importance.

The first, "government," (in the sense of governing or controlling pupils), did not itself actually produce moral development; it was merely a necessary precondition if moral development was to occur at all. In Herbart's view, the child had to learn to sit still if he was to be able to listen to the teacher. He had to be taught not to climb the neighbor's fence to pick the neighbor's flowers and fruit. Young children would have to be controlled in this fashion even if there had been no question of moral education. Their "wild impetuosity" required bridling if they were to live with each other and the rest of the world.

Herbart agreed with the pedagogical and social tradition concerning the necessity for government of this sort, and he acknowledged its basic importance. But he felt that once the concept was clear, anyone used to associating with children would have little difficulty with government. He included discussions of it in his educational works primarily because he felt his readers would expect a comprehensive treatment of pedagogy, of which government was an indispensable, if minor, part. In his opinion the important points for the teacher to remember were not to confuse government with discipline and not to use government when the child was mature enough for discipline to replace it.

As is evident from this possibility of confusion, government and discipline possessed many points of similarity. For example, both could and often did involve identical means. The distinction between them lay in the teacher's intention, in the use he was trying to make of whatever he did. Take the instance in which the teacher reprimands or punishes the child. As part of government, the teacher intends these actions simply as efforts to restrain the child, to keep him from doing again what he should not have done. By this exercise of government, the teacher, by conditioning, merely deters the pupil from being bad in the future, but he has not thereby rendered the child's will more moral.

In relation to discipline, however, the very same reprimand or punishment is intended for a very different purpose. It is to show how a will (the teacher's) sensitive to the moral law would regard the pupil's behavior. In this way the pupil is shown how his own "commanding will" (that which incorporates the moral law) should regard action that is produced by that part of his will determined by his desires and inclinations. In this context the imposition of the punishment is intended as a lesson in the first ethical idea, "inner freedom," a demonstration of how a moral will should judge a given action.

Thus discipline in Herbart's scheme was the direct influence of the teacher's will or character upon the pupil's will—by means of admonitions, reminders, the force of example, and other techniques that would develop and strengthen the pupil's own will. Since discipline actively and positively helped develop the moral will in the pupil, it should replace the more negative and nonconstructive government as soon as the child was mature enough to profit from discipline. Government alone, Herbart thought, could not build moral character since it was based on a will other than the child's own.

But discipline with its examples, models, and admonitions could benefit the child's moral will only after that will was somewhat developed. For example, the child must have reached the stage of passing moral judgments on actions before he could benefit from seeing proper examples of such judgments as models for his own. He had to have made moral choices and moral commitments before he could profit by the teacher's use of discipline in holding him to them. Discipline, in Herbart's view, could not implant the will; it merely guided and strengthened it. Chronologically, therefore, discipline did not merely come later than government; it also had to follow slightly behind "instruction," for the latter directly built the "circle of thought" and thereby the feelings, desires, and the will. Once instruction had made a beginning, however, then discipline could collaborate with it in molding the child's will along the desired lines.

Instruction was, consequently, the dominant member of the pedagogical triad. Its distinguishing characteristic for Herbart was that a "third something" was put by the teacher between himself and the pupil. Instead of working directly on the pupil's will, the teacher presented some "object" (a leaf, a story, a problem), as the object in which instruction was given. To present something to the pupil's attention was "to instruct."

According to Herbart's psychology, the contents of mind, the feelings, the desires, and the will were all built out of presentations. To control presentations was, therefore, to control to a considerable extent the resulting nature of the mind, the character, and the will.

For Herbart, therefore, the theory of instruction was the theory of what objects should be exhibited to the child, in what way, and in what order if they were to produce the proper kind of presentation—a presentation that when assimilated by the child would eventually produce the desired sort of will.

Yet Herbart saw the educator as confronted by a bewildering confusion—by a vast array of potential objects of instruction with varying utility for establishing the various moral ideas within the child. As indicated earlier, he felt that the only way out of this confusion was to look at the child as he came to the teacher and to ask what was feasible. To raise this question was to narrow sharply the field of realistic choice.

Herbart saw the child as a creature full of force and energy, undirected and uncontrolled, striving to go many different ways all at once. The child had no real will, but merely a wild impetuosity stemming from the whim or desire of the moment. To such a being, most of the ethical ideas seemed to Herbart inapplicable.

The only relevant idea was "perfection" inasmuch as it too concerned strivings or thrusts of power. But even its three aspects (intensity, extension, concentration) were not all relevant in the moral education of the young child. "Intensity" seemed to Herbart primarily the result of the child's constitution; some children were simply born with stronger wills than others, and education could have relatively little effect. Since intensity was one of the preconditions for "concentration" and since in any case concentration seemed to demand considerable maturity in the pupil, this third aspect of perfection also seemed inappropriate as a starting point for education. So by elimination, "extension" remained as the initial aim of instruction—to lure the student's will in as many different directions as possible—the more, the better. Or, in Herbart's pedagogical terminology, the aim of instruction at the outset was to arouse "many-sided interest."

In his ethics Herbart had specifically stipulated that extension of the will or even the whole idea of perfection was not in itself an adequate canon of morality. It was good as far as it went, but it was always to be limited and controlled by the other basic ideas. Similarly, in pedagogy, the arousal of many-sided interest was not to be viewed as the sole and complete end of moral education but only as the necessary first step.

But the world is full of potentially interesting things. The teacher needs some way of classifying them so that he can talk about them in general terms and can make sure that at least the major types are represented in his pupil's regimen. It is futile to talk about many-sided interest without some idea of how many "sides," so to speak, there are.

In attempting to make such a classification, Herbart was certain that there were several wrong ways that were to be avoided. One was to lose sight of "interest" in "the interesting"—to attempt to classify interesting things rather than interests themselves, a morass from which Herbart felt the teacher would never emerge. A second unsatisfactory method was to classify by subject-matter, cataloging things, phenomena, or methods according to the "science" to which they belonged. Since in moral education knowledge of the sciences was to be merely a means of arousing interest rather than an end for instruction to attain, use of this classification could easily confuse the teacher (and the pupil). Finally Herbart considered absurd any attempt to classify either objects of instruction or interests according to the mental faculty involved. He felt this way because he believed the faculties were mere figments of psychologists' imaginations.

He preferred to produce a more complicated but, in his opinion, more useful classification of interests and objects of instruction in the form of a multidimensional matrix. To evolve this table he went back to what he considered the two great sources of the contents of mind: experience (*Erfahrung*) with things and association (*Umgang*) with other human beings. These suggested his two major classes of interests, those of "knowledge" and those of "sympathy," each of which had three subclasses. The first subclass under knowledge Herbart called "empirical" interest since it had to do with knowledge gained through direct experience with things and their qualities. But certain other knowledge about the manifold of things is not given by direct experience alone; it requires something more. This knowledge of the great uniformities—species, classes, theories, laws, and so on—involves rational speculation in addition to experience and hence constitutes the second subclass of interests, the "speculative." Finally, as we saw in Chapter II, Herbart felt that experience with certain things (such as landscapes or works of art) evoked the judgments "pleasing" or "displeasing." This fact produced his third subclass among the "knowledge-interests": "taste," dealing with aesthetic relations.

In contrast to "knowledge" and its three subdivisions, the second major class of interests was "sympathy," also with three subdivisions. Paralleling the empirical interests, there was "sympathy with mankind," that is, with individuals met through direct association. Analogous to the speculative interests that dealt with something more than the things of direct experience, Herbart suggested "sympathy with society," that is, with larger groups not directly so experienced. Finally, the third subclass of the interests of sympathy covered the relations between mankind and society on the one hand and the supreme being on the other, "religion."

The six subclasses (empirical, speculative, taste; sympathy with mankind, sympathy with society, religion) were always Herbart's major scheme for classifying interests. Many-sidedness of interest was to involve all six types and also as many distinct interests as possible within each type.

But a scheme for classifying interests was not in itself adequate to guide instruction. The manner of instruction was also to be considered. Here Herbart saw three main types. First, instruction could be "purely presentive." That is, though casual experience with things and association with people would have brought to the student's attention many items of potential interest, instruction had the responsibility for introducing him to many things he had not happened to encounter and hence might miss completely in the ordinary course of events. These the teacher was to present as vividly and interestingly as possible. They could be objects, stories, works of art—anything new to the pupil's experience.

But whether the pupil had already become familiar with the object as the result of experience outside the school or whether presentive instruction had first acquainted him with it, Herbart's instruction had two other primary modes: analytic and synthetic.

Analysis took an object familiar as a unit and analyzed it into its parts. For example, a machine like a clock could be broken down into its components, or a piece of music analyzed into its melodic and harmonic voices. In synthesis, however, a familiar whole was shown as itself a part of some larger group or entity, a relation with which the student was probably not familiar. For example, the house cat was revealed as one of the vertebrates or mammals; the student and his family were placed in the larger context of the community and the state. Although Herbart believed that the mode of analysis was usually appropriate before that of synthesis, he did not demand the sharp serial ordering of them espoused by some of the later Herbartians.

This effort to aid the student in moving from wholes to their parts and from wholes to still larger units had its origin in what Herbart seems to have felt was the major problem of learning. Daily experience gave knowledge, but not organized knowledge. The task of instruction was to enable the student to organize what he knew. Not only were inchoate masses of knowledge useless for cognitive thought; more important, such bits and pieces did not build those vast, unbroken circles of thought that Herbart saw as the only basis of moral strength of character.

Much of Herbart's pedagogy, consequently, was devoted to enabling the student to assimilate his knowledge in adequately organized form. He saw as the basis of this operation what he considered the mental equivalent of respiration, an alternation between "immersion" and "reflection." In immersion the pupil concentrated on a single object or concept to the exclusion of everything else in an effort to see it clearly as what it was. In reflection, without losing this clear conception of the object, the student was to connect it in an orderly fashion with other things related to it. In short, instead of a mishmash of information, Herbart wanted the student to possess a set of crystal-clear items combined in an orderly array. The test of whether the student had attained this end was whether he could move back and forth across the parts of this conceptual structure without becoming either vague about the particular items or confused about their mutual relations.

This alternation between immersion and reflection was further developed in Herbart's famous four steps. From time to time he used different names for the various steps and sometimes he assigned somewhat different tasks to them. (As a result of this confusion, his later followers produced many variants in the number, names, and functions of the steps—as we shall see.) For Herbart himself, the commonest names were "clarity," "association," "system," and "method"; and their functions can be stated in this way: The student should *clarify* a concept, and then *associate* it properly with other related concepts in a *system* structured by explicit *principles* (method).

The first step, clarity, was related to that "clarity and distinctness" that Herbart's logic sought to give to concepts. In this step the pupil was to observe precisely the qualities and characteristics of a given object or concept. This concentration on the single object was, of course, immersion; the other three steps dealt with parts of the other process, reflection. Association linked the now clarified concept to others related to it. But such relations are part of a system or taxonomy of some kind, and such systems are built on principles of similarity or difference, dominance or subordination, and like principles. Obviously these last three steps are all mutually involved. Association of this sort is possible only within a system, and "method" focuses on the principles that generate the system. Thus the principles (method) and their system are already operative if association is to be possible. These steps were sequential only in that they gave the order in which the student's attention was to be focused on various aspects.

The student was, for example, to be shown an insect (e.g., a termite) or a gas (e.g., neon). In clarity he was to note its qualities; then in association he was to associate it with related things. But things possess many different qualities on the basis of which they can be associated. A termite, like a spider, is small and, like a worm, lives in wood. Neon, like oxygen, is colorless and, like mercury, is fluorescent. In this way one could build a system on principles like size, habitat, color, and so forth. To a certain extent, Herbart was prepared to accept systems of this sort at the elementary stages. But by and large, he would have wanted termites first to be associated with other insects and then to be incorporated into the system represented by the phylogenetic tree and its "method." In general the teacher could, of course, lead the pupil to the proper associations through the particular materials he used and the order in which he presented them. Thus he could tend to ensure that ultimately bats would be associated with whales and not robins and whales with bats and not barracuda. The pupil who had "learned his lesson" would have a precise knowledge of many varied items and of the principles relating them directly and indirectly to each other; that is, he could move up and down the phylogenetic tree, or, in the case of our other example, he could move freely over the periodic table of elements.

The significance of this procedure in the light of Herbart's psychology was noted in Chapter V. If a new presentation was not locked into its appropriate place in this way, it would simply be thrust below the threshold of consciousness by alien apperceptive masses. The guest at a tea or a cocktail party will swiftly depart if he finds no one he knows and cannot join any of the various groups. Consequently the conscientious hostess is careful to introduce him to other guests, suggesting possible ties of common friends, common interests, common backgrounds, and similar links. Basically the role of Herbart's teacher in presenting new material was the same.

Combining all the preceding classifications into a multidimensional grid (the six types of interest, the modes of instruction, and the steps) the teacher would have, in Herbart's opinion, a map of instruction in which everything would find its proper place. The teacher could present a large number of objects to the child to interest him and "set him in motion"; yet no hodgepodge, but a well-organized circle of thought would emerge because each item would have been put into its proper place and treated in the appropriate fashion.

So far we have considered only one aspect of one basic ethical idea, extension, in regard to perfection of the will —the idea that Herbart thought most accessible to the young child. And certainly that idea, because of its relation to the development of many-sided interest, dominated much of Herbart's program. But as the child matured and as government, discipline, and instruction had made their contributions, the child became ready for the other ideas. So, for example, Herbart was inclined to believe that even if left to themselves in favorable circumstances children would evolve for themselves the concepts of "right" and "requital" and become sensitive to these ethical ideas. Similarly, the child, through observation of his family, his teachers, and other adults in the community would have begun to acquire those moral standards requisite for "inner freedom." But how instruction would go about supplementing and developing these beginnings can probably best be seen by looking at the general kind of course of study Herbart used himself and recommended to others.

·VII·
Educational Program

How Herbart himself went about the business of teaching is pretty well known to us from a variety of sources. First, the *Reports to Herr von Steiger*, dating from the very beginning of his career, give us parts of a detailed account of the programs he arranged for his young charges in Switzerland. Second, Herbart filed an annual report with the Prussian Ministry of Education on the pedagogical seminar he conducted during his entire stay at Königsberg; and in 1831, when the continuation of the seminar was in question, both Herbart and his assistant, G. F. Taute, wrote unusually detailed accounts of what pupils in the seminar were taught. Third, in his pedagogical and psychological works, he often suggested and explained the use of particular bits of material.

In various places in his works Herbart used different categories for classifying subject matters. Probably the most illuminating was that which began by dividing subjects into the "mathematical" and the "historical." These two classes were then further subdivided. The mathematical included mathematics and the natural sciences. In terms of the kinds of interest involved, these mathematical subjects were directed primarily toward the "empirical" and "speculative"; in terms of the ethical ideas, they furthered extension of the will as part of the idea of perfection. The "historical" subjects included foreign languages, history, and geography. In regard to the interests, these historical subjects focused primarily on the three concerned with "sympathy"; they furthered all the moral ideas. A sixth subject, composition, was of a rather different kind, representing what Herbart sometimes called the "heterogeneous" studies. These did not serve moral education particularly; they appeared in the program primarily because competence in them would be expected of any child who had had schooling. These six subjects, then, (mathematics, natural science, history, foreign languages, geography, and written composition) were usually the main components in Herbart's actual programs, though other subjects such as music were sometimes included.

These offerings were rather standard fare in the programs of Herbart's time. What sharply distinguished his programs from the others of his day were the new purposes for which the traditional subjects were taught, the way in which they were handled, and the point in the child's education at which they were introduced.

Herbart emphasized these six subjects because he thought that, if properly taught, they could make a greater contribution than any others to moral education. As he surveyed the education of his day, he found them, unfortunately, not merely poorly taught, but taught at such a point in the child's development and in such a way as to deprive them of all their potential utility for moral education.

The study of mathematics and science, in Herbart's opinion, ought to have promoted that many-sided interest inherent in the idea of perfection. But in the gymnasium of his day, work in mathematics was regarded chiefly as preparatory and prerequisite for more advanced work in mathematics at the university. Herbart failed to see, consequently, how such instruction could be anything but a waste of time for the many students who did not continue their math there—to say nothing about the large number of gymnasium students who did not go to the university at all. Certainly the prevailing type of instruction seemed to him unlikely to be the kind that would most arouse and sustain interest in the student not naturally interested and gifted in mathematics. If success in arousing and sustaining interest was to be achieved, he felt that mathematics could come alive for the nonspecialist only through its applications, especially those to astronomy and mechanics. Yet to be able to use mathematics in this way the student would need more calculus than was usual but less work on some of the traditional topics.

Herbart attempted to work out a math course that fulfilled this need. As a result, in the Königsberg seminar he usually taught the mathematics to the pupils himself; his student-teachers, trained in the traditional way, were simply not up to doing the kind of job he wanted done. In his own way, then, Herbart introduced a "new math" and, according to the reports of the examining committees, achieved very impressive results. Yet, needless to say, the majority of teachers preferred to go on as before.

As we saw in the preceding chapter, work in math and natural science afforded the easiest example of the application of the "steps" to the teaching process. The teacher would present a mathematical or a natural object, and the pupil would be asked to observe closely its qualities and characteristics. Initially the instruction would probably be in the analytic mode, since it would begin with an object already familiar to the child and would analyze it into its elements or major characteristics. For example, in this first step, "clarity," the child at the outset would already be familiar in a vague way with "triangles," but he would not have observed them closely enough to have noted the characteristics on which identification of them as isosceles, scalene, and so on would depend. In this emphasis on scrutinizing single objects, Herbart was following the lead of Johann Heinrich Pestalozzi's "exercises in perception" and was at one with Louis Agassiz's repeated command to his students, "Look at your fish again."

But Herbart felt that Pestalozzi had not gone far enough. There was always the danger that the student would be left with nothing but a batch of close observations. As a result, he insisted on the addition of his next three steps so that ultimately a classification of those carefully scrutinized mathematical or natural objects would be obtained. In noting characteristics and in developing classifications, he acknowledged the usefulness of standard technical terminology ("isosceles," etc.) and existing systems of classifications. Yet he feared lest the teacher fall into the trap of teaching terminology for the sake of terminology or systems for the sake of systems. Technical terminology as a useful shorthand and extant systems as well-considered and viable organizations of knowledge were to be servants, not masters. The aim of instruction here was not to have the child come to know specialized terms or elaborate classifications as such; he was to make his perceptions clear and organized. This difference in purpose was alone sufficient to put Herbart at odds with the education of his time.

The work in the "historical" studies (foreign languages, history, geography), though also designed to be interesting and hence to help in perfection of the will, was directed primarily toward the other ethical ideas, to which mathematics and natural science were less applicable and useful. Herbart held no brief for history as chronicle, had no philological interest in languages, and no love for geography as a mere catalog of strange peoples and places. These subjects were to be studied because of the contribution they could make to moral education and studied in the way that would maximize this contribution.

The point can be seen most clearly in the use Herbart made of the classical languages. Latin and Greek were, of course, major subjects in the primary and secondary education of Herbart's time. Though he retained them, he played ducks and drakes with the customary purposes and procedures for teaching them. While the student normally began with Latin, Herbart insisted that Greek should come first. The study of each customarily began with a detailed and rather prolonged introduction to the forms and the syntax; Herbart wanted the student to get ahead into the literature as soon as possible. As a result he started the child on the reading of Homer's *Odyssey* after a very minimal preparation in Greek. And the purpose of this reading was not to master the morphology and syntax of Greek or even to learn the story; the aim was ethical, not philological.

To possess "inner freedom," for example, the child had to have a "commanding" will equipped with moral standards. The student could acquire these standards in various ways. He took them over from his family, teachers, other adults, and his peers; but he could also acquire them by reading. Similarly, the child could sharpen these judgments and perfect his ability to apply them by judging the events of his daily life; but he could also pass judgments on historical and fictional characters. This is the point at which reading the *Odyssey* became important. Herbart felt that for the earliest stages in developing and practicing the moral judgment the narrative of the *Odyssey* was superior even to daily life. Simple childlike characters confronted simple crises within a very simple culture. This material seemed to him a veritable five-finger exercise for elementary moral judgments, since the child had to · pass rather obvious judgments on cases lying well within his capacity, particularly within the range of moral problems he was likely to have encountered himself by this early age. In Herbart's opinion, there was only a brief span in the child's life during which he could profit most from this experience. Consequently Herbart was prepared to juggle the entire foreign-language curriculum in order to have the boy read the *Odyssey* at the age when he could most profit from it morally. In the usual curriculum the *Odyssey* came too late.

This use of the *Odyssey* typifies Herbart's use of all the historical materials. Historical characters and events also offered an admirable exercise ground for the passing of moral judgments. The child could learn in a variety of situations what is was to be brave, loyal, trustworthy, and the rest.

In fact, the work in history and foreign languages was tightly interlocked in several respects. As part of the work in Greek, the child read the histories of Herodotus and Thucydides; in Latin he read those of Livy and Tacitus. All four are, of course, primary historical sources for the periods they cover, and through reading them the child was getting historical as well as moral education. This is a point to which we shall return shortly. For the purposes of moral education, however, Herbart found in the accounts of Herodotus and Livy that same naiveté that commended the *Odyssey* to him as a workbook for developing and using moral judgments.

As the course of history moved on, civilizations and situations became increasingly complex and increasingly similar to those in which the boy would find himself. In this way the chronological sequence provided a series of exercises graded in order of increasing difficulty and leading ultimately to the sort of milieu in which the student himself would endeavor to lead the moral life. Herbart's hope was that the boy see a wide range of human motives and human conditions as depicted by poets, historians, and other portrayers of human nature, and that he incorporate into his own will the acceptable standards that he thus encountered.

The second stage of the language program illustrates another feature of Herbart's educational scheme. In this phase, after completing the *Odyssey*, the child returned to the detailed study of Greek grammar and to a reading, in the Attic dialect, of the more usual "introductory" authors, such as Xenophon. Herbart realized, both as tutor and as director of the seminar, that his pupils would sooner or later reenter the standard educational stream and would have to be able to hold their own with students who had had the customary philological drill. This phase of his program kept his pupils from losing all contact with standard educational practices. Similarly, the reading of the classical historians like Herodotus, in addition to giving practice in making moral judgments, provided his students with the sort of knowledge the regular schools labeled "ancient history." But emphasis on this sort of knowledge of languages and of history was, as far as Herbart was concerned, largely a concession to the fact that his pupils would move back into the usual programs of the day. This sort of erudition was merely a side-issue, not the main event. Since the pupil did have to learn this material, Herbart hoped that he would at least master it more easily and more efficiently because of the interest and competence he had acquired by reason of his introduction to it through Herbart's system.

The third phase of the language work was more in line with Herbart's interest in moral education. In this third phase (after reading the *Odyssey* and after the grammatical study and reading of Xenophon), the child read in the original Greek some of the shorter Platonic dialogues. In the first phase, the pupil had encountered in the *Odyssey* the sorts of motives and problems with which he was probably already familiar, and he was able to analyze and judge them for the most part by means of the intellectual and moral resources he already possessed. In this third stage, in the more profound treatments of moral issues by Plato (and in Cicero's *Concerning Duties*, the equivalent in the study of Latin), the student met problems that he probably had not confronted before, and he learned about arguments and complexities that were new to him. In this way his moral horizons were to be widened. A parallel increase in difficulty arose in the historical materials of the modern periods as the situations became more complicated and diffuse.

Geography, the third of the "historical" studies, Herbart considered the most difficult to teach effectively and, consequently, the study usually taught worst. In his opinion even Pestalozzi had been guilty of allowing the study of this subject to degenerate into a recital of the names and locations of strange lands and their inhabitants. Herbart, however, saw geography as potentially the great comprehensive and integrative discipline for the study of mankind in diverse cultures and physical conditions. To offer instruction at this level, the teacher would need, Herbart thought, the most ample intellectual resources and would continually draw on them all. But if rightly taught, geography offered the greatest variety of moral situations, moral standards, and moral judgments as well as the widest field for the development of all the classes of sympathetic interest.

The sixth subject, written composition, was not wholly unrelated to the other five even if it was labeled a "heterogeneous" study. Like many teachers of composition before and after him, Herbart was convinced that adequate composition was possible only if the student had something to write about and if that something was worth writing about. To meet these conditions, Herbart postponed the work in composition until the student had read the Plato and the Cicero. The student's papers could then be about the important moral issues and problems he had encountered there. But from Herbart's point of view the benefit of this procedure did not lie simply in the fact that the student acquired as an essay subject a worthwhile topic about which he knew something. Moral instruction also benefited. In these compositions the pupil made a written record of some of his moral analyses and judgments. Thus two advantages would be gained: his thought would be rendered more precise by being written down, and a record of it would be available to himself and his teacher for later comparison in attempts to chart his progress in moral development.

Even this slight amount of detail about the general content of Herbart's practical program should not cause us to lose sight of his major aim in all this. The student was to see situations to which moral judgments were applicable; he was to become acquainted with a selected group of moral standards in addition to those with which life in his home and community had already familiarized him; he was to get some practice in applying these criteria to historical and fictional situations of increasing complexity. As the outcome of this educational process, the student was to be skilled in applying the appropriate criteria to a wide variety of volitions and actions.

Up to this point the discussion has not involved Herbart's psychological machinery, and usually Herbart himself did not adduce it in connection with his practical programs. It can, however, be brought to bear. An obvious example would be the reenforcement of the moral standards through vaulting and pointing. Once a mass of presentations constituting such a standard was present in mind, it was continually made sharper and brought higher above the threshold of consciousness as new presentations from outside, representing relevant situations, pulled up or "made to rise" time after time those members of the old group that were most like them. With the passage of time, then, the standards became more clearly defined and more readily available. This result is precisely what the "commanding" will required.

From the foregoing account of Herbart's educational theory and practice, the reasons why they had so little impact on the education of the day should be apparent. Herbart was interested only in moral education, and he designed his program to produce it. Now, morality is a fine goal for education in that it is on the side of righteousness and a noble thing to talk about. But, as usual, parents, teachers, and political states were not primarily interested in it, if indeed they were interested in it at all past the level of talk. Parents wanted their children to be prepared to take good jobs or to enter the university. The state was interested in securing loyal subjects and socially and economically competent citizens. To be sure, both parents and state would be pleased if the students were *also* moral; but Herbart's almost exclusive emphasis on moral development must have seemed to many of them like carrying a good thing too far.

Contemporary teachers were subject to these same wishes and pressures. Probably more important, following Herbart's program would have compelled them to change their usual practices and habits and exposed them to the insecurities of attempting something for which their training and previous experience had not directly prepared them. And the fear that their pupils would be inadequately prepared in the traditional subjects must have been a very real one. Some teachers did, of course, adopt Herbart's scheme in varying degrees, but because of the monolithic nature of the theory it was hard to take parts of it without clearly distorting the general doctrine.

Finally, Herbart's emphasis on individualized instruction did not fit in with the requirements of the expanding schools of Prussia and the other German states. The application of discipline involved a one-to-one relation between the teacher's will and that of the pupil. Likewise, if one took the doctrine of apperception seriously, building a proper circle of thought required that the teacher know with considerable specificity what was in the particular apperceptive mass of an individual pupil at a given time.

Each new presentational mass had to be added properly to the specific one already existing in mind. It was for these reasons that the household tutor with a few children in his charge always remained for Herbart the pedagogical paradigm and that the students in his seminar always worked with five or six pupils at most, never with a class. But individualization of this sort was clearly impossible in the expanding schools of the time.

Since for these and similar reasons Herbart's theory and practice had relatively limited applicability as it stood, the subsequent history of the doctrine is an account of the efforts to modify the "systematic Herbart," whom we have seen up to this point.

·VIII·
The Unsystematic Herbart

The discussion thus far has presented Herbart's educational views as if they were integral parts of his total philosophic system simply because Herbart himself always insisted that they were. But the nature of Herbart's system and his own use of it seem to invite or even demand skepticism on this point. Consequently the century and a quarter since his death has produced a variety of views that question the alleged relations between his pedagogy and the rest of his system or that alter these relations in various ways, chiefly by cutting the pedagogy off from different parts of the system. These inclinations to modify the systematic structure have usually been occasioned by educational, social, political, or philosophical developments or have at least received reenforcement from them.

Efforts to modify the systematic nature of Herbart's educational thought that are specifically associated with Herbartianism, the educational movement bearing his name, will be the theme of some subsequent chapters. This chapter is concerned with a wider topic: the general motives and the specific grounds that many students and critics of Herbart have had for questioning whether there actually are close ties between his educational thought and the rest of his system and for undertaking to minimize or deny any such ties.

Major motives for this sort of interpretation have been the general unpopularity of philosophic "systems" on the grand scale and also the recognition of the weakness or obsolescence of particular parts of Herbart's scheme. As a result, those friendly to Herbart have apparently believed that to link his pedagogy to the rest of his system was to condemn him to the opprobrium more recently directed at "system builders" or to expose his educational thought to the kind of fate that has befallen his work in metaphysics, psychology, and ethics.

Their reasons for thinking that if Herbart's pedagogy is to be saved it must be freed from the rest of the system are understandable. Since the latter part of the nineteenth century, metaphysics of any sort has tended to be not merely unpopular but actually suspect. Even for those prepared to consider metaphysics at all, Herbart has not been a major figure. Though his metaphysical views are still cited in the histories of metaphysics and of general philosophy, the sections are brief and in small type. His ethical views, likewise, strike many modern thinkers as quaint. The rise and swell of experimental psychology have led many critics to reduce Herbart's status in that field also to at best the role of interesting and suggestive forerunner; they do not see him, as they see Wilhelm Max Wundt and Gustave Theodor Fechner, as an early bearer of the true gospel. If Herbart's educational doctrine is tightly cemented to its alleged metaphysical, ethical, and psychological foundations, but these are seen as eroded away by the advancing waves of thought, analysis, and inquiry, the educational doctrine can hardly stand firm, and it too becomes little more than a shattered ruin to be visited occasionally by curious antiquarians.

In consequence, those wishing to rehabilitate Herbart as an educational thinker or seeking what is "living" in Herbart's thought have felt under some pressure to divorce his educational views from his work in these other fields and have thus portrayed him as unsystematic. These approaches have examined his educational principles and doctrine in isolation and presented them as the wisdom of an intuitive, experienced, and thoughtful teacher and teacher of teachers. Or they have emphasized "the youthful Herbart," stressing the principles and practices of the *Reports to Herr von Steiger,* written when Herbart was a private tutor, or his early educational writings that reflect the influence of Pestalozzi.

His apparently systematic quality can then be minimized in various ways: as merely an effort to render education a sufficiently respectable branch of philosophy for it to be cultivated at a German university—or as an unfortunate consequence of his interest in these other fields, which made him see them as more relevant to his educational thought than they in fact were—or perhaps as complete delusion.

Yet this mode of treatment has its own difficulties. Isolated insights remain at best isolated insights. The admonitions, devices, and experiences of the master teacher have severely limited utility when they are severed from any consideration of the end they are to serve, from any theory of that learning process they are to promote, or from any concept of the human personality they are to affect. Those of Herbart's maxims that are established as valid on the basis of other, later theories or investigations have nothing but antiquity to commend them above the statements formulated by the later theorists or investigators. Picking away at the Herbartian corpus for nuggets of truth seems as much an antiquarian pastime as crawling about the ruins of a presumed system that has been demolished.

One's judgment of these general issues is naturally affected by one's assessment of the more specific grounds for doubting or ignoring the relations of pedagogy to the rest of the system. The more important of these points have already been noted, but they merit reconsideration here.

To begin with metaphysics, certainly pupils, teachers, and objects of instruction were never treated in a metaphysical fashion in the pedagogical works. The chief relevance of metaphysics to pedagogy lay in its furnishing the basis for psychology—by positing the soul as a real and establishing its self-preservations as the sources of the presentations and hence as the ultimate ground of those matters with which pedagogy was primarily concerned, that is, the circle of thought and the character. Even this indirect connection of metaphysics to education through psychology was slight, for the presentations as they appeared in Herbart's psychology showed little if any trace of their metaphysical origin. And since Herbart intentionally isolated metaphysics and ethics from each other and hence precluded any influence of metaphysics by way of ethics, the bearing of metaphysics on pedagogy is solely through this indirect connection by way of psychology.

Within psychology itself, moreover, there is good cause for asking whether this metaphysical grounding made any difference to Herbart when he functioned as a psychologist rather than as a metaphysician or epistemologist. The answer seems to be: almost no difference at all. Herbart, in his abstract mathematical treatment of the presentations as forces, distinguished among them primarily on the basis of their being "stronger" or "weaker" and "similar" or "dissimilar." His "mechanics" describing the interplay of presentations rests almost exclusively on these categories, and yet these distinctions were made on the basis of common experience, not metaphysics. For example, a loud noise produced a stronger presentation than a soft sound; colors were like each other, but colors were different from sounds. In short, the relations of psychology to metaphysics were rather slight and, as far as developments within psychology were concerned, unimportant.

The relations of Herbart's psychology to his pedagogy should be closer and in a sense they were. But these relations can be better assessed if compared with those of pedagogy to the other science bearing directly on it, ethics.

Certainly, of all the parts of Herbart's general system, his ethics was the one connected most directly and obviously with his pedagogical theory. At the most general level, Herbart's pedagogy was designed to make the pupil moral rather than learned, skilled, patriotic, or wealthy. What was more, this morality was at least partly specified by his five basic ethical ideas; and each procedure and object of instruction was judged on the basis of the contribution it could make either to morality in general or to the development of one or more of the ethical ideas specifically. Even the subjects that seemed to be ethically neutral (like mathematics) were justified on the basis of the contribution they made either to many-sided interest as part of the ethical idea of "perfection" or to that knowledge of the world requisite if the good will was to be effective. In short, ethical considerations did determine the end and through it the form and content of Herbart's pedagogy, and the ethics involved was that of Herbart.

Compared to that linkage, the psychology-pedagogy relation was much less obvious and explicit, at least at the superficial level. In the pedagogical works the explicit references to psychological theory are much less frequent than those to ethical theory. And in both explicit and implicit references, the pedagogical material was used to illustrate or suggest psychological theory. It was not the other way around; psychology was not used to predict or explain the pedagogical phenomena. In his pedagogical works Herbart argued for the most part from the familiar experience of those who have taught—the distilled wisdom of countless generations of schoolmasters—not from psychological theory. In his defense it can be argued, of course, that he foresaw his audience as an assembly of pedagogues, a group more likely to be persuaded by wisdom won on the "firing line" than by high-flown psychological theories. Furthermore, at least when the *General Pedagogy* appeared, his psychological ideas had not been published and perhaps not much worked out. Yet there is in turn a counterargument to this latter point in that the very late *Outlines of Pedagogical Lectures* made no greater use of the psychological apparatus though it made even more explicit use of the ethical theory than had the *General Pedagogy*.

Probably a fairer estimate is obtained, however, if one looks at the general principles underlying the pedagogy rather than at specific references and inferences. In this larger sense Herbart's psychological ideas indubitably permeated the whole fabric. His pedagogy aimed at producing the good will within the child, and instruction was for him the main division of pedagogy because it managed the presentations and thereby not merely the cognitive thought of the child but also his will. It was this conviction that made much that would otherwise have been mere book learning in his educational programs serve moral ends. Had Herbart believed that the will was an independent force or faculty rather than an ultimate product of the mutual interactions of presentations, much —one is tempted to say all—of Herbart's pedagogy would have been different. (The tendency of the later Herbartians to divorce the will from the circle of thought is a prominent feature of their doctrine that makes it appear a strange successor to Herbart's own views.) At this general level, Herbart's psychology was indeed a major determinant of his pedagogy.

But at the level of more specific educational principles,

the importance of the relations between psychology and pedagogy is much less apparent. A rather typical example is the multidimensional grid used by Herbart to classify the objects of instruction. There the basic point, Herbart's theory of mental respiration or the alternation between immersion and reflection, could of course be justified on the psychological ground that the "vaultings" must be given time to subside if the more precise "pointings" were to be maximally effective. And if the general theory of this respiration is seen as based on this psychological justification, then the more specific parts of this process, such as the "steps," can be also viewed as psychologically necessitated.

Yet the reader of Herbart's pedagogical works is likely to wonder whether, in this case at least, Herbart actually moved from psychology to education rather than in the reverse direction. This contrary motion would be seen as arising out of Herbart's interest in the organization of knowledge as one of the great aims of education. As we have seen, the major function of instruction was to help the child organize the knowledge he already had and to give him new knowledge to add to this structure in order to build those large, well-articulated circles of thought that Herbart prized. To this end the four steps merely enabled the child to see each bit of information as it was and to put it in its proper place in the framework. Once the four steps were evolved, then the first could have suggested immersion; the other three, reflection. In this way, working with a very minimal logical apparatus inherent in the organization of knowledge, Herbart could have produced these major principles of his pedagogy even if he had never thought of vaulting and pointing. Of course, this argument would run, once he had thought of them, he could connect them with the mental respiration and the steps.

The preceding points have been matters on which Herbart had rather distinctive personal positions. The actual state of affairs is even more uncertain in regard to those points in Herbart's pedagogy that had been familiar in education thought for centuries. A typical instance of such a hoary principle is his emphasis on the pupil having models to imitate—his teachers and parents, historical personages, and literary characters. In terms of the psychological theory, such vivid examples of moral behavior constitute a strong and coherent mass of apperceptions, which produces marked vaultings and pointings; for example, a new moral example would further strengthen the moral maxims and the awareness of the moral law already present because of these models in the pupil's circle of thought. But there is the other possibility that Herbart might actually have adopted this procedure of numerous other educational writers from Plato on and might merely have felt happy when the device proved to fit his psychology. Here again there is basis for asserting that Herbart's psychology at most confirmed or justified his educational practices but did not predict or dictate them.

Grounds for doubting the importance of psychology in the actual shaping of Herbart's educational views can also be found within the pedagogical works themselves. As noted earlier, the *Reports to Herr von Steiger* advanced many of the educational principles that Herbart was to espouse for the rest of his life. But at the time the *Reports* were written, his system, especially the psychological parts of it, was presumably undeveloped, to say the least. In regard to principles appearing in the *Reports*, consequently, it might seem to be a clear case of "pedagogy first, psychology later." Yet here again, judgments must be less than conclusive. Herbart had to have an idea before he wrote it and published it. In all probability he had been juggling parts of his system in his head for many years before they took sufficiently coherent and rigid shape for him to be prepared to say that he had a system or to feel ready to write out a part of it. In other words, the time and order in which we learn that Herbart had ideas certainly do not necessarily conform with the actual chronological sequence in which he had these ideas and used them.

The points cited in this chapter—and others like them that could have been added—all indicate that there are good grounds for suggesting that Herbart's educational theory was largely independent of his metaphysics and his psychology, or at least can be treated as if it were. When evidence of this sort is combined with the more general considerations noted at the beginning of this chapter, it is no wonder some students of his doctrines have taken the view that his thought was actually less systematic than he always alleged. A plausible case can be made out in part on the side of either "systematic" or "unsystematic." By this point in the book the reader has seen much of the evidence pro and con. Though he has not seen all the evidence and perhaps not enough to make his own decision, he should at least be in a position to realize how tentative the judgment either way must be.

Consideration of the possibility that Herbart was not systematic has at any rate prepared the reader for the sort of thing that happened in the different varieties of Herbartianism long after Herbart's death. All of them tended —in varying ways, to various degrees, and for various reasons—to divorce pedagogy from other parts of the system. Metaphysics was the most easily and commonly dispensed with. Ethics was often retained in the sense that "morality" was still asserted to be the end of education. But since the basic ethical ideas, particularly in their exact bearing on instruction, were often ignored and since the will was made independent of the circle of thought, ethics usually became much less explicit and much less important than it had been for Herbart. Psychology was that part of the system most generally retained. But the machinery of apperception was seen as limited to the structuring merely of cognitive thought, not as the building of moral character; and pedagogy and psychology sometimes went their separate ways. In short, even if Herbart had been systematic, the Herbartians changed that situation once and for all.

·IX·
Herbartianism

Any account of Herbart and his work is woefully incomplete without some notice of the later educational movement that flourished under his name, Herbartianism. The reason is simple. Had it not been for the rise and spread of Herbartianism, we would be much less interested in Herbart, for he had personally generated very little fame or influence. Yet the amount of Herbart involved in Herbartianism may be likened to a few bricks in a large educational edifice, and certainly the most influential and controversial parts of Herbartianism, the items that made it a lively educational movement, have very slight connection with Herbart's own theory and practice.

Herbart had relatively little influence during his lifetime and in the quarter-century following his death. To be sure, H. G. Brzoska, who was once his assistant in the pedagogical seminar at Königsberg, probably perpetuated some of his work through his book, *The Necessity for Pedagogical Seminars at the University*. Likewise, Volkmar Stoy, who had also been a student of Herbart's, was a fairly important figure in German pedagogy and preserved and disseminated some of Herbart's ideas.

The true father of Herbartianism, however, was not Herbart but Tuiskon Ziller. Ziller originally took a great many ideas from Herbart, but it was his extended development of only two or three of them that came to constitute the chief elements and characteristics of Herbartianism. Consequently, although Ziller began by transmitting Herbart's ideas, in the process of elaborating a few of them to fit his own purposes and situation he ultimately produced an educational program linked only tenuously, at these two or three basic points, to Herbart's own thought. What is more, at best these points had been for Herbart only minor ones in his theory and practice.

Although Ziller had not been a student of Herbart's, he came to know his work from the most authoritative sources. Yet even then he had a general interest of his own in view. Born in 1817, the son of a pastor in a village near Meiningen, he had entered the University of Leipzig to study law. Family circumstances prevented his completing his work, however, and he returned to teach in the gymnasium at Meiningen, thus becoming involved and interested in the practical problems of education. He had also developed a desire to benefit humanity, particularly to improve the lot of the lower classes. In view of this interest, when he returned to Leipzig about 1850 to complete his studies, he soon gave up the law and devoted himself to a more general course in philosophy and philology.

His work in philosophy brought him into contact with two professors who were major authorities on Herbart. One was M. W. Drobisch, who during Herbart's lifetime had been his closest student and collaborator in the fields of psychology and metaphysics. The other professor was G. Hartenstein, a historian of philosophy who was then beginning to publish the first edition of Herbart's collected works. If anyone ever had a chance to learn about Herbart from impeccable sources, it was Ziller, and he took advantage of the opportunity.

What most attracted Ziller to Herbart's thought was apparently the idea that character could be built (and even to a degree rebuilt) by structuring the circle of thought properly. Certainly this would be one way of regenerating the lower classes. And as far as Ziller's general educational interests were concerned, Herbart's ideas seemed to him also applicable as an appropriate way to educate the masses of German citizens.

But Ziller soon made two additions to Herbart's doctrine that became almost the defining characteristics of all later Herbartianism. He introduced the "concentration centers" and the "culture epochs."

A concentration center was a general topic on which the work of a whole school year focused. Ziller undoubtedly felt that in introducing the concentration centers he was simply following Herbart to the point that the latter should have reached himself had he developed his own principles to their proper conclusion. Herbart had made

much of the "unbroken circle of thought, close-knit in all
its parts." Only such a unified circle of thought could produce the desired unity of consciousness and integrity of
character. But Ziller, as he looked at Herbart's programs,
either as set forth in his books or as actualized in practical
programs, felt that the necessary unity was certain to be
lacking. The work of a given year would be fragmented
into a set of subject matters or a series of topics unless
some specific effort at integration was made. The purpose
of the concentration center was, therefore, to produce a
unified circle of thought by concentrating on a single
major theme or topic.

The concept of the culture epoch also had some roots
in Herbart's thinking, though it had been familiar for
many centuries before him. Essentially this idea is the
educational equivalent of "ontogeny recapitulates phylog-
eny"; that is, just as the embryo retraces the biological evo-
lution of the species, so the child's education should move
through the major stages of man's intellectual and moral
development. To be sure, Herbart had seen chronological
sequence as the desirable organization for some parts of
education (though he was opposed to it for other parts),
but certainly he nowhere specified an exact set of stages as
the Herbartians were to do.

The ideas of concentration centers and culture epochs
could, of course, be easily combined. The culture epochs
could simply serve as the concentration centers. Consequently, much of the later Herbartian literature pivots on
three questions: (1) Should there be concentration centers? (2) Should the culture epochs be used as the concentration centers? (3) If the answers to the first two

questions were in the affirmative (as they were for most Herbartians), what were the proper culture epochs to be used as concentration centers? Another vast mass of the Herbartians' literature then presented the actual course outlines and classroom materials to be used in teaching the selected concentration centers.

In view of these preoccupations of the Herbartians, it is important to remember that at best Herbart himself had merely *implied* the need for concentration centers and that his nearest approach to using the culture epochs was to emphasize the desirability of the *chronological* organization in treating *some* topics. Insofar, then, as the movement connected with his name emphasized the concentration centers and the culture epochs—and certainly they were two of the three or four distinguishing characteristics of "Herbartianism"—the relation of Herbart's own theory and practice to this subsequent activity of his alleged followers was necessarily slight.

The specific directions taken by the work with the culture epochs in the Herbartian literature can be understood only within the later social and cultural context in which these developments occurred. Since several factors were involved with which Herbart had not been concerned, the Herbartians' efforts to cope with them necessarily produced ultimate educational products remote from anything Herbart himself had used or envisaged.

Probably the most fundamental force was the effort of the Herbartians to work on a larger scale than had Herbart. His practical activities, apart from tutoring, had been limited to his small pedagogical seminar and to consultation concerning the programs of some local schools. As indicated earlier, his effort always was to individualize education in the manner of the private tutor; and the complete application of his principles for discipline and instruction demanded highly specific knowledge of the individual pupil and personalized planning for him.

But by the time of Herbart's "followers," the private tutor, if not an anachronism, represented a minor sector of the educational enterprise in contrast to the ever-expanding schools and school systems in the latter half of the ninteeenth century. At the very least, the Herbartians' program was going to have to be viable in these larger educational units. If in addition their programs could help coordinate and standardize those still larger organizations of regions or nations, so much the better.

A second major factor was that during much of that century the elementary schools of the German states were denominational—Lutheran or Catholic. Unlike many lands where friction between church and state was intense, in German-speaking territory there was satisfactory cooperation between these two powers, at least as far as elementary schooling was concerned. As a result, the culture epochs that were chosen had to be acceptable and, preferably, appropriate to *religious* schools.

The context within which the Herbartians worked also tended to fix at eight the total number of school years to be dealt with. Herbart had planned the training given children by his seminarians as leading into the last year of the gymnasium. But even in his time he was impressed by the number of students in the gymnasium who did not belong there. Its program was intended to prepare students to enter the university; but because it was the prestigious secondary institution, many families sent their sons there even though they had no intention of later sending them to the university. The *Burgerschule,* intended in Herbart's day for the general education of that part of the populace not aiming at the specialized training offered by university work, was scorned as plebeian. By the time of the Herbartians, political states were placing increasing emphasis on the education of the citizenry, and many of the German Herbartians were interested in upgrading the *Volksschule* and developing it into the major instrument for mass elementary education. Since this school covered an eight-year sequence, the problem was to provide eight appropriate concentration centers. (The American Herbartians, the only other national group that can be treated in this volume, likewise had to deal with an elementary school with eight grades.)

The foregoing facts suggested to Ziller his original plan, which was followed by much of German Herbartianism throughout its history: the eight culture epochs used as concentration centers should be those of Biblical history. This sequence would include the patriarchs, judges, and kings of the Old Testament and the life of Christ and the history of the early church from the New Testament. This ecclesiastical history could be extended to include the life of Martin Luther and the Reformation —a possibility more welcome to the Lutheran than to the Catholic institutions, needless to say.

At the practical level, however, to begin children's general schooling with the Biblical patriarchs proved unsatisfactory. The names, the customs, and the environment were all too strange to serve as materials for the very beginnings of the child's literacy. The Biblical epochs were consequently pushed back in the schedule and prefaced by two years of work in concentration centers more suited to the elementary years. The first year employed German folk tales and stories, which were sufficiently simple to be usable and which could also be partially justified on the ground that they stemmed from a primitive state of Germanic culture. The second year was generally centered on *Robinson Crusoe*, because it had been recommended as suitable for elementary work by no less a figure than Jean Jacques Rousseau in *Emile*, and because it too could be viewed as representing a rather simple level of culture. The Biblical epochs could then follow in order, beginning with the third year.

But the sequence—folk tales, *Robinson Crusoe*, Biblical epochs—was, of course, not the only way of filling the eight years. With the continuing rise of nationalism, particularly after the unification of the German states under Bismarck, sequences based on German rather than on Biblical history were proposed. These could replace or could run in tandem with the Biblical sequence. Variants of this national sort were especially attractive to countries that wished to inculcate their own cultural and national history or where the religious instruction inherent in the Biblical sequence was suspect or forbidden. Each country could substitute its own stories and heroes and could follow the progress of history from its own national perspective. Thus the American Herbartians could use American stories, substitute *Hiawatha* for *Robinson Crusoe*, and

close the series with a center on the founding of the re-
public.

The following table illustrates the general scheme:

YEAR	BIBLICAL HISTORY	GERMAN HISTORY
1		Epic fairy tales
2		*Robinson Crusoe*
3	The patriarchs	Thuringian sagas
4	The judges	Niebelungen sagas
5	The kings	The German kings (e.g., Barbarossa)
6	The life of Jesus	Life of Luther
7	The apostles	The spread of Protestantism
8	The Reformation	Nationalization of Germany

Not the least virtue of agreement on specified culture
epochs was the possibility it offered for unifying school
systems by producing the basic outline for a regional or
national course of study. This agreement could also lead to
the standardization of the materials used for each center.
Along these lines, Wilhelm Rein, the last of the great
Herbartians, took the lead in producing a series of eight
volumes, each of which provided the materials necessary
for teaching the concentration center of one year.

In addition to the use of the concentration centers and
the culture epochs, another distinguishing characteristic
of the Herbartians was their emphasis on the theory of
apperception, and especially on the "steps" as involved in
it. At these points their relation to Herbart's own theories
is much closer than in the case of the concentration centers and the culture epochs, but even here the changes
were fairly drastic.

The general theory of apperception held that new

presentations would simply sink below the threshold of consciousness unless they were attached to similar presentational masses already present in mind. As we have seen, the last three steps of Herbart's four were designed to effect this linkage.

Herbart's own operations in regard to the steps suffered from some very obvious shortcomings. First of all, his terminology was far from catchy and was actually opaque. The words "clarity," "association," "system," and "method" simply did not point very clearly to what each involved.

Second, Herbart himself did not always use the same names to refer to the steps. This fact is not so much a source of confusion to his followers as it was a ground for asserting that he was not satisfied with his names for the steps and would himself have been willing to change had he hit upon a better set. This shifting of terms is, however, also related to another matter to which we shall come in a moment, the fact that several rather different operations are sometimes included within a single step.

Third, the steps were part of a fairly complex, multidimensional model including also the types of interest and the modes of instruction. Anyone trying harder than Herbart to make the model popular would be tempted to simplify it drastically. Incorporation of at least parts of all this material into a fairly short and uncomplicated arrangement—especially by modifying the steps to include at least parts of these other distinctions—was an attractive kind of simplification.

Fourth, Herbart tended to assign to some of the steps

—especially the fourth, "method"—a variety of functions. The fourth step was a particularly likely victim for this procedure since it (making explicit the principles that generated the "system" of the third step) was already implicit in that third step as well as in the second, "association." As a separate step, therefore, "method" involved nothing more than making explicit to the student the principles of classification that had already been operative. Consequently, Herbart tended to mention other useful activities that could be performed by the student at this stage, such as practice in running through the system now that the principles had been learned, or practice in applying the system in the classification of appropriate new items. These activities were perfectly defensible pedagogically, but they were something different from what had originally been included in "method."

In view of these facts, it is scarcely surprising that the Herbartians devoted so much effort to changing the names, number, and functions of the steps. Since a detailed account would be inappropriate here, a couple of examples will suffice to show how all four points played parts in the subsequent developments.

Ziller was the first to make the steps five in number, substituting two of the modes of instruction, analysis and synthesis, for the first step, "clarity." In this way he omitted or at least blurred what Herbart had meant by clarity, but he did manage to incorporate the instructional modes of treating wholes, on the one hand, as consisting of related parts and yet, on the other hand, as being in their turn parts of larger wholes.

But the steps are best known to Americans in the version of Wilhelm Rein:

> Preparation (*Vorbereitung*)
> Presentation (*Darbietung*)
> Association (*Verknüpfung*)
> Generalization (*Zusammenfassung*)
> Application (*Anwendung*)

His version clearly reflects the influences of all four of the considerations mentioned above. His terms indicate plainly the chief thing to be done by the teacher at each step. Furthermore, in this terminology they have a certain face-validity and plausibility as an analysis of the stages in the teaching process quite apart from any pedagogical or psychological theory. Any teacher, whether Herbartian or not, would understand them at sight and probably feel that they made sense. Undoubtedly much of the "Herbartianism" to which we find casual reference amounted to little more than the fact that teachers used the steps in lesson-planning, whether or not they knew anything more about Herbart and Herbartianism than that sequence.

It is also clear from Rein's version that the Herbartians were still following the general doctrine of apperception. In "preparation" the teacher led the child to recall the particular material with which he was already familiar that would be relevant to the new material he was about to encounter. In "presentation" the teacher introduced the new subject matter in as interesting and vivid a way as possible. "Association" and "generalization" (the latter, as the German indicates, being a "pulling together" of the material in a systematic fashion akin to Herbart's step of "system") then followed—and in this respect followed Herbart's procedure.

Finally, in "application," one of Herbart's functions for his fourth step was given the full place. Having evolved a general concept, for example, the student was to practice fitting new material into it.

In these elaborations of the steps Herbart would certainly have recognized his own doctrine, though he would have been surprised to see so much emphasis given to what had been merely one part of his own theory.

The most fundamental change, however, was that for most Herbartians instruction was no longer "educative" in Herbart's strict sense of that term; it no longer led to the formation of moral character through building the will. The aim was purely cognitive. The pupil was to be able to organize and structure his knowledge, with special emphasis on the development of general concepts or general ideas. But for most of the later Herbartians, the will was no longer the creature of the presentations. Consequently, though the end of education was claimed to be "morality" in some vague sense, instruction could no longer build moral strength of character in the way that Herbart had sought to build it. Apperception and the steps became merely a general theory of cognitive learning usable in all sorts of specializations. Herbart had not been opposed to such learning; he simply was not interested in it. Once instruction was declared unable to do what he had wanted it to do, he would have resigned from the local Herbart society.

·X·
American Herbartianism

American Herbartianism was such an odd phenomenon in so many respects that it is surprising that it has received so little attention from the educational historians. Although the main outlines are clear enough, detailed studies could shed light in many shadowy corners.

By the 1880s American education at all levels from the kindergarten to the graduate school, if judged by any quantitative and qualitative criteria, was burgeoning. One area in which improvement was being sought and won was that of advanced training for professors in higher education. American colleges were endeavoring to transform themselves into universities on the German model. But since the activities of the German laboratory and seminar were then the paradigm for the scholarly world, many young American scholars still made the pilgrimage to the original shrines.

Students of most disciplines had a considerable range of choice among the German universities, even though in a given field the professor and the work at one or two institutions might be particularly famous. But the student who wished to pursue the advanced study of education as a field of inquiry rather than psychology, history, or some other more traditional field, found his choice much more restricted. There were two "real" chairs of pedagogy in Germany (as distinct from mere teacher-training programs), those at Jena and at Leipzig. Both of these were occupied by Herbartians, with Stoy and then Rein at Jena and Ziller at Leipzig. As a result, traveling American pedagogues, if they were not merely doing the grand tour but undertaking serious study or working for a degree, were fairly certain to enroll at one or both of these universities and thus to become acquainted with German Herbartianism.

Three young men from Illinois State Normal made the hegira. Though Charles DeGarmo and Charles McMurry ultimately took their degrees from Halle (in 1886 and 1887 respectively), both studied at Jena, and the younger McMurry brother, Frank, took his degree there in 1889. The three then returned to the United States to make careers of importing Herbartianism. The United States with its expanding schools and normal schools was ready to welcome a "scientific" pedagogy, which offered not merely a wealth of organized practical materials but also an impressive theoretical foundation laid by a real German philosopher.

German educational thought was not new to America. Henry Barnard in his *American Journal of Education* had endeavored to inform his compatriots about European developments in general, including Herbartianism; and W. T. Harris as superintendent of schools in St. Louis and later as U.S. Commissioner of Education was doing much to publicize the Hegelian point of view. But in DeGarmo and the McMurrys, Herbartianism found three unusually energetic and determined promoters.

Returning to America, DeGarmo published in 1889 his book on "Herbartian principles," *The Essentials of Method;* and this and his later *Herbart and the Herbartians* (1895) were two of the major vehicles of Herbartian thought in America. His series of articles in 1891, "The Herbartian System of Pedagogics," in the first volume of the *Educational Review,* is noteworthy on two counts. First, it was a major effort in a general educational journal to inform American readers in English about German Herbartianism as distinct from the adaptations that he and the McMurrys were making in their books. Second, it initiated the role that the *Educational Review* was to play for a decade as a major organ of the American Herbartians. Though its editor, Nicholas Murray Butler, was not a Herbartian, he was generally sympathetic to the movement during this period, and more Herbartian material appeared in the *Review* than in any other national journal. In addition to his original contributions, DeGarmo himself translated and stimulated others to trans-

late several of the major works of the German Herbartians
as well as some of Herbart's own pedagogical writings.

Meanwhile the McMurrys had not been idle. Charles
had published his *Elements of General Method* in 1892
and collaborated with Frank in *The Method of the Recitation* (1897). Other American Herbartians like C. C.
Van Liew were also publishing, and the books of the English Herbartians were being published simultaneously in
the United States. As a result of all this activity, within
little more than a decade almost two dozen major Herbartian books became available to American educators. No
other movement or school of thought could lay claim to an
equal number of volumes—to say nothing of showing
equivalent quality.

Nor was such success as American Herbartianism
gained due merely to its poundage of printed materials. A
Herbart club and other societies and reading circles were
organized. Finally, in 1895, DeGarmo and the McMurrys
organized the National Herbart Society, with Nicholas
Murray Butler, John Dewey, and other prominent figures
serving with them on its executive council. Not that
Dewey ever espoused Herbartianism. In fact, he used the
society's *Yearbooks,* to which he contributed, mainly as a
medium to spread his own ideas. But in Butler, Dewey,
and the others the Herbartians found conspicuous educators who were prepared at least to have their names associated with the movement in an official capacity. Similarly,
Colonel Francis Parker, though no True Believer, was always sympathetic to the movement because he felt it a
useful stimulus to American educational thought. This
list of educators who for various reasons associated them-

selves with the movement could be extended, but the total effect was to give the American Herbartians a prominent platform from which to preach their gospel.

Another factor working for the Herbartians was the simplicity and definiteness of their doctrine. The concentration centers and the 1-2-3-4-5 of the steps demanded no great thought and appeared eminently "practical" and "helpful" to teachers of teachers. In this respect Herbartianism stood in marked contrast to such competitors as G. S. Hall's "child study." In teachers' minds there was some feeling that after one had "studied the child," the sticky question of what to do on Monday morning still remained. In contrast, the Herbartians told them what to do in some detail.

For a period of at most fifteen years American Herbartianism was a lively enterprise, probably reaching its peak about 1896. Then the decline set in rather rapidly. The *Fourth* and *Fifth Yearbooks* of the society (those of 1898 and 1899) were scarcely Herbartian at all, and then, about 1899, the society perished; however, it was revived in 1902 as the National Society for the Scientific Study of Education, with Herbart's name notably omitted. Another index of the decline of the movement is the drastic pruning of much of the Herbartianism from the later editions (1903) of the two books by the McMurrys. As a theoretical movement producing publications, speeches, and general excitement, American Herbartianism was dead by 1905.

To ask how influential it was during its heyday is to raise a question for which we have too few of the raw data for a competent answer. Certainly it made reputations; it was much talked about; the Herbartians were recognized as a forceful group at meetings and conventions. But how much difference did it make, if any, in how teachers taught?

Here we confront a fact illustrating the usual lag in education. As has been said, American Herbartianism was practically dead as a theoretical movement by 1905. But the last edition of Charles McMurry's *The Elements of General Method* did not appear until 1903, when the movement had already lost most of its impetus. Yet this book sold about 70,000 copies, and was reprinted as late as 1923. *The Method of the Recitation* by both McMurrys was revised that same year and managed to sell about 23,000 copies. DeGarmo's *Essentials of Method* was kept in print until 1934 and sold about 33,000 copies, and Adam's *The Herbartian Psychology as Applied to Education* sold more than 18,000 until it went out of print in 1936. Obviously the publishers did not keep them in print as a public service or as a favor to educational historians. Copies were being used as texts, and there is some informal evidence that many educators who went through teacher-training programs as late as the 1920s used one or more of them. Courses of study and teachers' manuals also may well have contained stronger or fainter traces of Herbartianism in some form even though the texts were not used. On these points formal studies are still lacking.

The question why Herbartianism dropped so rapidly and completely from sight can receive only some partial answers. As my colleague J. W. Getzels has suggested to me, it is probably significant that the full name of the society was the National Herbart Society for the Scien-

tific Study of *Teaching*. Yet at approximately the same
time as the society died, Hall was still plugging *"child
study,"* Dewey was writing *The CHILD and the Curriculum* (1902), and E. L. Thorndike was beginning his
studies of *learning*. For a good many years "the teacher"
and "teaching" were to be unpopular topics compared
with "the child" and "learning"; and "teacher-centered"
was the properly opprobrious epithet to hurl at the Herbartians. Not only did the question "How do people
learn?" seem to have to come before the question "How
can people be taught?"; the answer to it seemed to many
to incorporate automatically the answer to the other question. When occasionally someone did deign to talk about
instruction as did Henry Clayton Morrison in his popular
Principles of Teaching in the Secondary School, his plan
for "science-type" instruction looked, to say the least, suspiciously like the Herbartians' steps.

The drive to make education "scientific" still continued, but as the mention of Dewey and Thorndike suggests, a number of other paths were now opening up that
educators could follow in their search for the "science of
education." As a result, the popularity of Herbartianism
would probably have tended to diminish in any case
simply as a result of increased competition.

But a stronger force than mere competition was operating against Herbartianism. The new experimental psychology of Wilhelm Max Wundt, Gustave Theodor
Fechner, and E. L. Thorndike was rising. Herbart himself
had believed that psychology should be empirical but not
experimental. His rejection of experiment does not seem
to have rested on the ground that this procedure consti-

tuted using people as "things" rather than "ends" or on any fear of deleterious results to his experimental subjects. Rather his position was more inherent in his fundamental view of the nature of the field. Had he believed in the faculty-psychology, he would perhaps have undertaken to make experimental studies of memory or reasoning or any of the others. But he did not regard mind as composed of faculties or capacities or separate abilities that would be isolated and studied; and his theory of mind as constituted by the interaction of highly complex and particularized masses of apperceptions did not lend itself to the simple, neat laboratory manipulations through which the experimentalists were seeking to give psychology a scientific base.

As a result, the advance of experimental psychology made that of Herbart and the Herbartians appear not merely old-fashioned but even unscientific. This latter verdict was a severe blow to a movement that, above all, had sought to found a scientific pedagogy on the basis of a scientific psychology. Because Herbartian pedagogy was linked so closely to what the Herbartians had developed as the theory of apperception and because this theory was not easily susceptible to experimental treatment, Herbartianism as a theoretical movement rapidly foundered on the rock of experimental psychology. Out of the wreckage a few pieces, like the use of the steps in developing general ideas, could stay afloat for several more decades as isolated procedures, but such unity as had been possessed by the "system," whether Herbart's or the Herbartians', was destroyed.

·XI·
The
Summing Up

Herbart was naturally gifted, and he constantly strove to exercise and develop his original talents. "Diligent" is a characteristic noted in the reports about him as a school boy, a theme for the eulogies at his burial, and an epithet frequently attached to his name in the intervening years.

This combination of endowment and effort brought him more than ordinary success. Professionally he was more than just another university professor of his day. He was extraordinarily popular as a lecturer. He published a dozen or so books. He held rather distinguished academic posts.

In personal relations, though the effects of his childhood experiences apparently always made these contacts difficult for him, he did achieve a happy marriage and found at least a small core of devoted friends throughout his life. His obstinacy in following his own course, a characteristic that he developed early as a defense against intense parental (particularly maternal) pressure, can also be seen as what he would have called "moral strength of character." A career marked by integrity, diligence, productiveness, and affection is more than is given to most men.

Yet there was a darker side to Herbart's life. His intense efforts to be creative in the fields of metaphysics, psychology, and pedagogy brought him much less fame than he had hoped to achieve, and even such success as he had won seemed likely to perish with him.

In metaphysics he was fated to seek distinction at the very time when Germany was producing her greatest crop of speculative thinkers: Kant, Fichte, Schelling, and Hegel. In addition to encountering this level of competition, Herbart, listening as usual to the beat of his own drummer, was completely out of step with this vanguard of the philosophic parade. As a result, he spent the mature years of his life at Prussian Königsberg while Hegelianism was almost the official philosophy of Prussia, and in the Golden Age of idealism he was propounding a realistic metaphysics and a mechanistic psychology. His metaphysics displayed considerable ingenuity, but even if it had been more adequate, it would probably have languished if only from isolation.

His efforts in psychology were more productive of students and followers than were his metaphysical doctrines. Yet many of these followers appeared only after his death, and most of them offered heavily "revised and amended" versions of his psychological views. Though historically we usually honor him for his opposition to the faculty-psychology and for his efforts to make psychology an exact science, to determine precisely how mind and personality are built up out of experience, and to give greater precision to the theory of the association of ideas by charting their exact interplay, these contributions were much less apparent and important to his contemporaries than to us. In his own day, his "mechanistic," "deterministic," and "antispiritual" views rendered him suspect.

In his pedagogy too he was out of step with the theory and practice of his day. At the very time when the schools and school systems of Western Europe were expanding and consolidating, he offered a brand of pedagogy most obviously applicable to the work of the private tutor. His theory was complicated and was difficult even for him to handle. Furthermore, he stressed principles, classifications, and general procedures intended to guide those who were as interested as he in thinking about education generally and in working out precisely what should be done in specific situations; he did not offer much in the way of pre-cooked and predigested programs and teaching materials adoptable by those interested in getting the maximum of help with the minimum of effort. In practice, his reforms were sweeping and demanded a complete reworking of the aims, organization, and content of teaching foreign languages, mathematics, and geography—to take only the major examples. His programs offered little that could be adopted piecemeal.

In short, at the time of Herbart's death, his success was limited and was less than he had hoped for or perhaps even expected. Actually he was scarcely even a likely candidate for posthumous revival. In fact, had the story ended at this point, the modern student of education would have heard little about Herbart. He is remembered in education primarily because of Herbartianism.

These pedagogical followers achieved greater success on his behalf (if indeed it may be called his) by making certain drastic changes in his theory and practice, with the amount of alteration increasing with the passage of time. For the most part they moved to the elementary level of education, thus avoiding the tradition and other demands of the secondary level. Here, usually by introducing the concentration centers and the culture epochs, they offered a full and detailed program, complete with course outlines and teaching materials for the classroom. Wherever Herbart's sprawling system appeared cumbersome, obsolete, or likely to provoke controversy, they minimized these relations or cut their versions of Herbart's pedagogy completely free from these encumbrances. By measures of this sort, the Herbartians managed to make their movement a major one in education for a half-century or so and thus preserved Herbart's name.

But because of these very changes, Herbartianism constituted a revival of Herbart's own theory and practice only to a very limited extent. True, there are connections, and Herbart's own work is partly relevant to consideration of the ideas and practices of the Herbartians, who usually tried to hand on as much of his original doctrine as they did not feel compelled to alter or to reject. Nonetheless, as a result of the changes wrought by the Herbartians, we find ourselves in the odd position of being interested in

Herbart primarily for reasons for which he actually was hardly responsible. That is, we tend to be interested in Herbart because of the tradition through Herbartianism; but much of the interest and excitement produced by that movement came from materials like the concentration centers, which have little direct connection with Herbart.

If, however, we disregard the activities and the materials of the Herbartians as merely perversions or deformations of Herbart's pedagogy and attempt to return to his original thought and practice, we then encounter those same difficulties in his doctrines that led to the Herbartians' changes. Furthermore, we can find little that is "living" or "useful" in Herbart's doctrines that has not already flowed in some form into the mainstream of education either through the Herbartians or through other channels.

In short, the relation between Herbart and Herbartianism is not what we might have expected. Herbartianism did not in fact represent the practical application or historical development of Herbart's ideas, nor did Herbart furnish much of the basic structure of that rather lively and fairly influential educational movement. The relation is much less direct and more complex.

In this regard the story of Herbart and the Herbartians is a fairly typical and well-documented example of what often happens in educational thought. A thinker evolves a set of ideas and practices, and through them he gains a certain amount of fame and influence. (Any educational reformer, of course, fails if judged by the standard of his own hopes and aspirations.) Then, more or less contemporaneously, he gains followers. These adherents usually begin by assimilating and disseminating the doctrines of their leader, Mr. X. But there are "errors" to be corrected, difficulties to be avoided, rough edges to be smoothed out. Then, too, situations change, and the original doctrines seem less applicable to new social and educational contexts. The followers also have ideas of their own. These they mix with what they think most valuable or useful in the original doctrine. Then we no longer have the "theory of Mr. X" but "the influence of X" or "Xism." As time goes on, the relations between Mr. X and Xism become more and more tenuous as the processes of altering, excerpting, and adding continue, until Xism often consists largely of matters with which X himself had no concern and may even include positions that he personally opposed.

Education is not of course the only field in which this process occurs, for it is a commonplace in the history of ideas; and Herbart was certainly neither the first nor the last educator to whom it has happened. His case is, however, a particularly nice example of the way in which time grinds the edges off once clear-cut ideas and tosses the transformed remnants onto the general pile of educational thought.

Bibliography
and Notes

COLLECTED WORKS

Hartenstein, G. *J. F. Herbarts Sämtliche Werke.* 12 vols. Leipzig, Ger.: L. Voss, 1850–52; 2d ed. 13 vols. Hamburg: 1883–1893.

Kehrbach, K., and O. Flügel. *Johann Friedrich Herbart, Sämtliche Werke in chronologischer Reihenfolge.* 19 vols. Leipzig and Langensalza, Ger.: Hermann Beyer & Söhne 1887 ff. Reprinted, Aalens Ger.: Scientia Verlag, 1964. Subsequent references to the *Sämtliche Werke* (SW) are to Kehrbach.

BIBLIOGRAPHIES OF HERBART AND HERBARTIANISM

Rude, A. "Die Literatur der Pädagogik Herbarts und seiner Schule" in C. Thilo, O. Flügel, W. Rein, and A. Rude,

Herbart und die Herbartianer. Langensalza, Ger.: 1897.

Schmitz, J. N. *Herbart-Bibliographie, 1842–1963*. Weinheim, Ger.: Julius Belz, 1964. (This volume is unfortunately much less comprehensive than the title alleges.)

Ueberweg, F. *Grundriss der Geschichte der Philosophie*. 13th ed. by T. K. Oesterreich. Basel, Switz.: Bruno Schwabe, 1951. Part IV, pp. 158–160, 362–373.

SELECTED GENERAL BOOKS ON HERBART

English

DeGarmo, C. *Herbart and the Herbartians*. New York: Charles Scribner's Sons, 1895.

Felkin, F. M. and E. *An Introduction to Herbart's Science and Practice of Education*. London: Swan Sonnenschein, and Boston: D. C. Heath, 1895.

German

Thilo, C., O. Flügel, W. Rein, and A. Rude. *Herbart und die Herbartianer*. Langensalza, Ger.: Hermann Beyer & Söhne, 1897.

Flügel, O. *Herbarts Lehren und Leben*. Leipzig, Ger.: B. G. Teubner, 1907.

Frizsch, T. *Johann Friedr. Herbarts Leben und Lehre*. Leipzig, Ger.: B. G. Teubner, 1921.

Weiss, G. *Herbart und Seine Schule*. Munich: E. Reinhardt, 1928.

CHAPTER 1   *Life*

The indispensable materials for the biography of Herbart are contained in *SW* XVI–XIX. These are the extant letters from, to, and about Herbart, plus certain other biographical source materials. Other important items appear in *SW* I, most notably the "Recollections" of Johann Smidt, Herbart's lifelong friend from university days on. Since Smidt served as an intermediary on some occasions between Herbart and his family and visited the older Herbarts at Oldenburg, Smidt's account throws unique light on Herbart's relations with his family.

In addition to the general works on Herbart listed above, all of which contain more or less extensive biographical accounts, see F. Bartholomaï, "Johann Friedrich Herbarts Leben," in his *J. F. Herbarts Pädagogische Schriften*, 7th ed. by E. von Sallwürk (Langensalza, Ger.: H. Beyer & Söhne, 1903). W. Asmus has begun a very detailed biography, "Der Junge Herbart," *Pedagogica Historica* I (1961), 1–38, 348–387; III (1963), 133–190, 420–474.

CHAPTER II *Herbart's System*

The account of Herbart's system in the text follows chiefly his own exposition of it in his *Lehrbuch zur Einleitung in die Philosophie*, SW IV, 42–49. The letter in which Herbart's friend C. W. Böhlendorff announced to another friend, J. G. Rist, that Herbart had found his system appears in SW XVI, 97.

The most extensive presentation in English of Herbart's system remains that of James Ward (s.v. "Herbart"), *Encyclopaedia Britannica*, 11th ed. (Cambridge, Eng.: Cambridge University Press, 1910–1911). A briefer one by Harold B. Dunkel appears in Paul Edwards (ed.), *The Encyclopedia of Philosophy* (New York: Macmillan, 1967), III, 481–484. Among the American histories of general philosophy, the best treatment is by B. A. G. Fuller and S. M. McMurrin, *A History of Philosophy*, 3rd ed. (New York: Holt, Rinehart and Winston, 1955).

CHAPTER III *Ethics*

The major text is Herbart's *Allgemeine praktische Philosophie*, SW II, 329–458. It has never been completely translated into English though parts of it are available in K. Price, *Education and Philosophical Thought*, 2d ed. (Boston: Allyn and Bacon, 1967). There are no monographs on the ethics in English, either originals or translations.

CHAPTER IV   *Metaphysics*

The relevant texts are *Hauptpunkte der Metaphysik*, SW II, 175–216; *De attractione elementorum*, SW III, 155–200; *Lehrbuch zur Einleitung in die Philosophie*, SW IV, 147–270; and *Allgemeine Metaphysik*, SW VII and VIII. There are no translations or monographs in English. Apart from Herbart's own works, the most useful book is M. Mauxion, *La metaphysique de Herbart* (Paris: Hachette, 1894); moreover, those who read French but not German can get a fair idea of the originals from Mauxion's translations and paraphrases.

CHAPTER V   *Psychology*

The three principle texts are the *Lehrbuch zur Psychologie*, SW IV, 295–379; *Psychologie als Wissenschaft*, SW V, 179–434, and VI, 1–340; and *Briefe über die Anwendung der Psychologie auf die Pädagogik* SW IX, 339–462. Of these texts, two have been translated into English: M. K. Smith, *A Textbook of Psychology* (New York: D. Appleton, 1891); and B. C. Mulliner, *The Application of Psychology to the Science of Education* (London: S. Sonnenschein, and New York: C. Scribner's Sons, 1898).

G. F. Stout, "The Herbartian Psychology," *Mind*, XII (1888), 321–338, 473–497, gives the most extended account in English of Herbart's general psychological position. In accord with the fashion of his day, he minimizes its metaphysical and postulational base, but he illustrates how a psychologist of that time would see Herbart's psychology as a psychology.

CHAPTER VI *Pedagogy*

All the major pedagogical works are available in English. The *Allgemeine Pädagogik* (SW II, 1–139) has been translated by H. M. and E. Felkin under the title, *The Science of Education* (London: S. Sonnenschein, and Boston: D. C. Heath, 1892). The *Umriss pädagogischer Vorlesungen* (SW X, 65–196) appears in A. Lange, *Outlines of Pedagogical Lectures* (New York: Macmillan, 1901). It also appears in the Felkins' *Letters and Lectures on Education* (London: Swan Sonnenschein, and Syracuse, N. Y.: W. C. Bardeen, 1898). Also see W. J. Eckoff's *The ABC of Sense-Perception and Minor Pedagogical Works* (New York: D. Appleton and Co., 1896).

The best of the books in English on Herbart's educational doctrine, in the sense that it puts the doctrine into the largest context of Herbart and the Herbartians, is the Felkins' *Introduction to Herbart's Science and Practice*. Also good within limits but somewhat colored by the views of the German and American Herbartians, respectively, are C. Ufer's *Vorschule der Pädagogik Herbarts: Ufer's Introduction to the Pedagogy of Herbart*, J. C. Zinser (tr.) (Boston: D. C. Heath, 1894); and C. DeGarmo's "The Herbartian System of Pedagogics," *Educational Review* I (1891), 33–45, 244–252, 453–462.

CHAPTER VII *Educational Program*

The available material on the Königsberg seminar is collected in SW XIV and XV. I have treated some of its difficulties briefly in "Herbart's Pedagogical Seminar," *History of Education Quarterly*, VII (1967), 93–101. Translations of the *Reports to Herr von Steiger* can be found in the Felkins' *Letters and Lectures*.

CHAPTER VIII   *The Unsystematic Herbart*

This general point of view is ably presented by C. Casel-mann, *Der unsystematische Herbart* (Heidelberg: Quelle & Meyer, 1962). Also relevant is B. Schwenk's *Der Herbartver-ständnis der Herbartianer* (Weinheim, Ger.: Julius Beltz, 1963). Also useful, particularly on the relation of the psy-chology to the pedagogy, is H. Ströhle's *Herbarts Psychologie im Verhältnis zu seinem Erziehungsideal* (Stuttgart, Ger.: C. Belser, 1903). This position has never been popular with the writers in English on Herbart, of which there have been few since the heyday of Herbartianism.

CHAPTER IX   *Herbartianism*

The indispensable source for materials on the concentration centers and the culture epochs is Wilhelm Rein, A. Pickel, and E. Scheller, *Theorie und Praxis des Volksschulunter-richts nach Herbartischen Grundsätzen,* 8 vols. (Leipzig, Ger.: Heinrich Bredt, 1881 ff.). In this compendium, Wil-helm Rein devoted each volume to presenting the material to be used in a single year of the *Volksschule.* His citations of the literature on the controversy are exhaustive, particularly in the successive editions of Volume I. Some of the contro-versy over the concentration centers as well as other aspects of Herbartianism has been translated by F. H. Hayward and F. E. Thomas, *The Critics of Herbartianism* (London: S. Sonnenschein & Co., 1903).

American readers will find illuminating two articles in the *First Yearbook of the National Herbart Society* (Normal, Ill.: Public School Publishing Co., 1895): C. C. Van Liew's "The Educational Theory of the Culture Epochs" and L. B. McMurry's "Correlation of Studies with the Interests of the Child for the First and Second School Years."

For biographies of the Herbartians and for Herbartian discussions of educational topics, a most useful source is W. Rein, *Encyclopedisches Handbuch der Pädagogik* (Langensalza, Ger.: Hermann Beyer & Söhne, 1903–1910). DeGarmo's *Herbart and the Herbartians* also gives some material of this sort in English.

CHAPTER X *American Herbartianism*

The major original works of the American Herbartians were noted in the text: C. DeGarmo's *Essentials of Method* (Boston: D. C. Heath, 1889) and his *Herbart and the Herbartians* (New York: Charles Scribner's Sons, 1895); Charles McMurry, *The Elements of Method* (Bloomington, Ill.: Public School Publishing Co., 1892); and Charles and Frank McMurry, *The Method of the Recitation* (Bloomington, Ill.: 1897).

The Americans also made available in English a number of German Herbartian handbooks popular at the end of the 19th century. In psychology they translated G. A. Lindner, *A Manual of Empirical Psychology*, C. DeGarmo (tr.) (Boston: D. C. Heath, 1890); K. Lange, *Apperception*, The Herbart Club (tr.) (Boston: D. C. Heath, 1893); and they produced J. Adams, *The Herbartian Psychology Applied to Education* (Boston: D. C. Heath & Co., 1897) and H. T. Luken's *The Connection Between Thought and Memory* (Boston: D. C. Heath, 1895), an adaptation of Friedrich Wilhelm Dörpfeld's *Über Denken und Gedächtnis*. (Gutersloh: Bertelsmann, 1866). In the field of pedagogy, they translated into English C. Ufer's *An Introduction to the Pedagogy of Herbart*, T. C. Zinser (tr.) (Boston: D. C. Heath, 1894) and W. Rein, *Outline of Pedagogics*, C. C. and I. J. Van Liew (trs.) (London: S. Sonnenschein, 1893).

I am indebted to Charles F. Wedon of D. C. Heath and Company and Miss June Meyer of the Macmillan Company for the publication figures cited in the text. Unfortunately the records of the other publishers of Herbartian books have been destroyed.

Index